Balboa Press books may be ordered through booksellers or by contacting:

Balboa Press
A Division of Hay House
1663 Liberty Drive
Bloomington, IN 47403
www.balboapress.com
1 (877) 407-4847

Because of the dynamic nature of the Internet, any web addresses or links contained in this book may have changed since publication and may no longer be valid. The views expressed in this work are solely those of the author and do not necessarily reflect the views of the publisher, and the publisher hereby disclaims any responsibility for them.

The author of this book does not dispense medical advice or prescribe the use of any technique as a form of treatment for physical, emotional, or medical problems without the advice of a physician, either directly or indirectly. The intent of the author is only to offer information of a general nature to help you in your quest for emotional and spiritual well-being. In the event you use any of the information in this book for yourself, which is your constitutional right, the author and the publisher assume no responsibility for your actions.

Any people depicted in stock imagery provided by Thinkstock are models, and such images are being used for illustrative purposes only.
Certain stock imagery © Thinkstock.

Print information available on the last page.

ISBN: 978-1-5043-2568-4 (sc)
ISBN: 978-1-5043-2570-7 (hc)
ISBN: 978-1-5043-2569-1 (e)

Library of Congress Control Number: 2014922813

Balboa Press rev. date: 5/6/2015

Our Grand *Journey* of *Self-Exploration*

Two Souls Journeying to the Great Beyond

Tara O'Toole-Conn

and the soul of Peter D. Conn

BALBOA
PRESS

A DIVISION OF HAY HOUSE

We dedicate the energy and love in this book to all souls willing to be touched by this information. Our profound lessons can bring greater spiritual awareness to those seeking the gift of expanding their knowledge of soul-to-soul communication, by merging the spirit and physicality.

Opportunities to find deeper powers within ourselves
come when life seems most challenging.
— Joseph Campbell

Contents

☙

Preface

I would never have called myself a writer, especially because my husband, Peter D. Conn was a professional writer most of his life. During our twenty-two-year relationship, I lived in the shadow of the success of his accomplishments as a writer. However, since the passing of my beloved Peter on November 2, 2013, I have had revelations that surprised me! I realized that the story about our spiritual journey over the past decade *wanted* to be told. I could feel that its importance was something that I owned, and it could not come into the world without coming through me. I followed my heart, knowing that my inspirations penetrated the profound calling of my soul — like sunlight percolating into the room.

At first, with an *urgency* in the early hours of the morning, I began to awaken to an inclination to write. Was this a voice inside of me telling me to explore this idea? My life had not always been about the soulful experience, even though there were many twists, turns, and synchronicities that showed up along the way. I felt this endeavor was a part of a dance of courage unfolding before me.

Since my husband made his transition, I have endeavored to move through a sea of sorrows, hoping to find islands of joy on which to rest and rejuvenate during the grieving process. Along the way, instead of just thinking about it, I chose to put my thoughts on paper. In doing so, I found myself weaving a path to writing about our grand journey over the past decade. I feel as though it assigned to me, and I recognize that I am the only one who can bring our story through and into the world. I believe we all have special and unique life experiences through which life lessons flow; there is something about the life lessons of our spiritual journey that wants to be written.

Reaching a decisive stage in my life's purpose, I chose to follow my soul's longings. At this point, I was not sure what I needed to navigate the deep waters of my spiritual self. I started writing about our journey when the pangs of bereavement began to reveal themselves. I began journaling about my irrepressible feelings of love for Peter, about our joyful times, and about how unhappy I was without him. My deepest feelings for Peter were the hardest to express verbally because these emotions were so much deeper than at the surface. With tears brimming in my eyes, I would write about the loss of his physicality and the fact that I felt even closer to him after his transition. This simple yet heartrending act of expression and creation made me feel better.

This experience has allowed me to reclaim parts of myself. It has made me aware of the certainty that I can no longer ignore Peter's passing. Ultimately, it has also blessed me with the opportunity to explore who I am now. As I continued to evolve beyond my identity of the past ten years, I found a breathing space with a renewed sense of purpose and passion. The pure experience of what I have come to call "our grand journey of self-exploration" was unquestionably the most important of my life. In this process, I grew. My life steadily developed as my grief grew more balanced with bouts of self-healing of these emotions, my mental stability, and physical wellness.

I explored what a life without Peter would be like. I tuned-in to myself to open up to a different vision of my future. At the same time, I recognized that my new sense of purpose landed me here on these pages, writing for the purpose of healing myself and helping others.

This newfound meaning and purpose compelled me to express the beauty of our miraculous journey. Had it not been for our profound lessons and the fullness of the love and empowerment we created throughout our journey, we could not have reached these new levels of understanding. It paved the way to a divergent lifestyle, and my health and happiness moved to a new intensity.

Acknowledgments

On behalf of my beloved husband, Peter D. Conn, I extend loving gratitude to our first channel/medium, Sally Baldwin. She brought great comfort and guidance to us while experiencing the struggles of searching for a new way to communicate. She spoke directly to our souls in a conversational way, and the energy exchange was of the highest order. She was truly an emissary of love between our world and the spirit world, bringing forth messages of enlightenment without which our soul connections would not be possible. *Our Grand Journey of Self-Exploration* would not be the beautiful creation that it is without our greater grasp of the spiritual realm and how it applies to life on Earth. We are profoundly grateful, and we love and honor Sally for this unparalleled gift of the spirit, and for paving the way for our ongoing spiritual unfoldment. After our beloved Sally had passed on June 6, 2012, we embraced the blessings of joy in our hearts when one of her protégés, Laura Mirante, Channel/Medium stepped in.

Laura Mirante brought a seamless connection to Peter and me during the last nine months of Peter's human life and after his transition to the spirit world. Through her gifted and masterful channeling, she brought to bear deeply profound experiences that advanced our energy to a higher and more fulfilling place. She revealed the song of Peter's soul regardless of the nature of the mood or vitality he was experiencing. She assisted Peter to open up from his heart and soul and view the wonderment of who he truly is as a spiritual being. We extend our profound gratitude and love to Laura for this immeasurable gift and the elegant way in which she supported us in shaping our experiences. Thank you, Laura; we honor you.

I extend our most heartfelt gratitude and love to our longtime friend, Beverly Dowdle, who gave us our initial introduction to channeling during a casual phone conversation as I lamented about losing Peter. My life changed when she said to me, "Oh, you can talk to him when he's gone!" She then referred me to Sally Baldwin. Beverly assisted us in a divine way to find who we were while going through a difficult time in a physical way. Without her willingness, we could not have shifted our conscious understanding of what it was we were doing. My sorrow and yearning associated with the loss of my loved one's physicality dissipated by her assistance and support that helped me to feel the insurgence of knowing this can be different. With deep affection and appreciation, thank you, Beverly.

With love and gratitude, I would like particularly to mention all the beautiful souls, too numerous to mention by name, who have supported our journey. They are caregivers, doctors and nurses, counselors, teachers, and friends that have given freely of their time, resources, and hearts. We offer a special thank you to Peter's dedicated massage therapist, Teresa Raque, for her faithful support, love, and friendship.

With deepest love, we especially extend our heartfelt gratitude to my precious sister, SuAna, and to Peter's beautiful and loving family members who enveloped us with love and support in untold ways, while sharing our grand journey.

My gratitude and congratulations go to the staff of Balboa Press, a Division of Hay House, for exercising the highest caliber of professionalism throughout the publishing process. I extend my gratitude to our editor, Dana Dyer Pierson, for her masterful editing and invaluable insight.

Thank you, Creator of the Universe, for giving us everything that we needed to let our words shine through.

Introduction

The energy of the universe permeates all objects and life forms on Earth. When we put good vibrations out, they will emanate back to us. If our thoughts vibrate energy for the highest good, the Earth's positive energy will rise to meet higher levels of spiritual consciousness. Inclined to extend the energy vibrating inside me, I chose to write our story. In sharing our grand journey of self-exploration, we will take you on a journey of the meaning of the wisdom and power of communicating through life soul-to-soul, whether your soul is in the physical or spiritual realm. Our spiritual journey has dramatically transformed my life and that of my husband. Our most profound lessons can serve others and bring peace into the hearts of those experiencing our same situation.

Our story begins shortly before 2003 and views a decade of life through illness and beyond — through the vast magic of Peter's transition to the great beyond, and communing soul-to-soul, here and now in spirit. There is a message here that gives voice to a deeper meaning of life beyond death. Our story stems from our spiritual ideal to which we are committed and for which we are following the call of our souls. The brilliance of our journey is in our ignorance prior to how Peter's illness triggered this kind of journey. Although the metaphysical principles of this story are different from what many may believe, we believe that it has the potential to be of profound significance to those willing to embrace our story and learn from the lessons. Its transformative nature will become a bridge for those searching to find encouragement to deepen their path to the spiritual dimension of life and the sense of knowing the depth of their soul.

Through our journey, we have grown in grand and glorious ways while, at the same time, Peter struggled with limitless courage and fortitude. While experiencing the complications of physical immobility and the inability to speak, Peter relinquished all resistance to his limitations. His ability to live in a state of surrender to his circumstances enabled us to reach higher states of spiritual awareness. Each step we took expanded our ability to believe what could be possible. The magic of this lies in the unexpected outcome after many years of illness. Without realizing the depth of how Peter surrendered to what is, I believe our book could not have manifested. For this, I honor him.

Through the courtesy of an 'excerpt' from a recorded, verbatim transcribed session of our communications while writing this book (channeled by myself as clairaudient on July 8, 2014), the following is a gift from Peter's soul awareness:

Peter: I love you, my dear, and I am so proud of you and what you are doing to connect us. We are writing a book, and I want to write the Introduction.

Tara: Peter, I understand you want to write the Introduction to our book, *Our Grand Journey of Self-Exploration*. Is the proposed title of our book still okay with you?

Peter: Yes, Tara, that's fine for now. I want to write the Introduction about how we came to this place in our spiritual development, and show people how to do this for themselves.

Tara: Certainly, Peter, please go ahead.

Peter: Our journey of self-exploration has been the most creative and magnificent experience I have ever known. The essence of what is in this book will perhaps shock you at first. I am here to tell anyone who is interested in learning from us, that this quest has been the most important adventure; not only of my past life with Tara, but of any of my past lives before this one. Know this from one who has never thought of himself as spiritual, or even practiced a religion or the belief in G-d. I come to you with the most authentic validation one possibly could bring through and into the world.

It's time for all souls to put aside any long-held beliefs that they are simply a human body traveling this lifetime without the counterpart of themselves, the knowledge of their soul that is within all of us. We can raise the spiritual consciousness level of the planet by developing our awareness of who we are, not only as a human being, but also as a spirit — the soul that we are, that never leaves us. At this point in my spiritual development, I find it unimaginable to live on the Earth without the soul aspect of who we are.

Tara and I know that we have much to share with the world by writing this book as a way of communicating soul-to-soul. With my deepest and most profound sense of who I am as a soul in the spirit realm, I offer this beautiful writing that Tara and I have compiled for your soul awakening with the knowingness that we can all communicate with our loved ones, in spirit.

  Tara: Peter, thank you. That is beautiful. I love you.

[End of session 'excerpt.']

Perhaps our story will transform your thoughts about the reasons why Peter and I took this journey. We shared a grand journey that tells of the synchronicities that reveal the message of finding peace and freedom from your ego. *Our Grand Journey of Self-Exploration* uncovers a startling message that has profound spiritual implications for us all. It is just the beginning, so we invite you to enjoy reading about how deeply meaningful and personal our grand journey can resonate for you.

Chapter 1

How We Met

In 1991, as I was searching for new employment, I accidentally dialed the wrong phone number from the phone book. After months spent at my precious mother's bedside during a long-term illness and her eventual death, I was in need of a new job. She lived in New Jersey, and I lived in Florida. The morning I received word that my mother was either having (or had just had) a heart attack, I immediately hung up the phone, and I placed a call to the emergency center in the area where my mother lived to dispatch an ambulance. That same evening, I walked into her hospital room, my heart filled with love and thoughts of finding precious moments with her while hoping to drown my fears that she was too ill to survive. My sisters and I stayed with our beloved mother throughout many days and nights, watching over her and spending those last few months together until she passed. When I returned home to Florida, my unplanned and extended hiatus gave way to the emergence of new circumstances for employment.

As I thought about my life and the overwhelming loss of my dear, sweet mother, I felt a change of sorts brewing inside of me. I had been working in law firms as a legal assistant for too many years, so the idea of working outside of an office and perhaps in the marketing field appealed to me. Instead of rooting out prospects on my own, I turned to the phone book for names of employment agencies to set up appointments. I dialed the only employment agency listed in the Yellow Pages, and a man named Peter answered the phone. I quickly realized that I had *not* dialed the employment agency as I had intended. At first, I thought I had accidentally dialed the wrong number. He continued that his company was not an employment agency and that the phone company inadvertently listed his company name under the heading of employment agencies instead of consulting firms. He added that he occasionally received calls like mine and that until a printing of the new phone directory, there is little he could do about it.

I apologized for interrupting his day. Before I could hang up, he politely asked me what kind of a job I was searching. I told him I wanted to work outside of an austere office setting, perhaps in the marketing field. I added that I wanted to meet new people. He explained that he was a specialist in strategic business planning and communications and that he prepared business plans and competitive proposals for a wide variety of private- and public-sector clients. Although he had never actively engaged in marketing his company since its inception in 1981, he had been thinking about it for some time now. He asked me if I would be interested in interviewing for the position. I resisted, saying that I did not know and that I would first want to believe in the product. We talked a bit more and agreed to meet for an interview. At that time, I learned more about his company and about how he had relocated to Miami, Florida, in 1978. The fact that we had both moved to the Sunshine State in the same year intrigued me. He moved from Kentucky, and I had moved from New Jersey.

On a trial basis, I agreed to work with this gentleman. He also had a condition for me, a request that I first take a personality screening to find out if we were compatible to work together in the business.

He explained that in the past, other employees he hired did not work out based on personality differences. I said that I did not mind being tested. Perhaps I would find out something about myself at the same time. After the screening, the counselor reported that he and I were perfectly compatible, and there was no reason we would not work well together. I began working with this man shortly after the day that I accidentally dialed the wrong phone number, and he eventually became my husband. Looking back, I believe that the first day we met in person, a commitment to being with him existed in my heart. We never stopped thanking Ma Bell for connecting us.

The scope and character of Peter's public life were far-reaching. Years after meeting him, I learned about his distinguished careers in newspapers and state government. After attending the University of Louisville, he became managing editor and print news journalist for his family-owned newspaper, *The Jefferson Reporter.* In the early 1970s, he founded and ran weekly newspapers in the US Virgin Islands. Later, in 1974, he was a public affairs commentator of *Prose and Conn* on WHAS Television and Radio in Louisville, Kentucky. He won a number of regional awards and two national awards for print journalism and two local Emmys for radio and television commentary. He later founded and published *Baby Times Magazine*, a national publication for new parents that won three national awards.

Peter did not have an interest in the supernatural or anything that transcended the laws of nature. He leaned toward metaphysical naturalism rather than supernatural concepts and religion. As a humanist, he looked to science rather than religion to understand the world. His sense of benevolence toward other human beings was huge in scope. He cared about and treated all human beings without distinction, and he demonstrated this in various government positions that he held. He had a great capacity for promoting concern for the welfare of others and the planet as a whole. His sensitivity to all lives did not exclude any person for their beliefs or religious practices.

Peter's role in Kentucky state government began when he was in his late twenties and first elected in 1970 as a Democrat from Louisville. As the youngest member of the Kentucky House of Representatives, he immediately drew attention to his campaign for greater openness in government, including personal financial disclosure requirements for elected officials. As Chairman of the House Committee on Cities in 1972, he oversaw a major Louisville home-rule measure passage.

Peter joined the administration of Governor Julian Carroll in 1975 as an executive assistant to the governor. From 1977 to 1979, he served as Secretary of the Department of Human Resources and earned national recognition for launching some of the first statewide programs of comprehensive care for the mentally disabled and emotionally disturbed youth. The passage of his auditing and budgeting reforms, coupled with the allocation of public funds programs were credited with significant savings in welfare and departmental expenditures.

Soon after Peter's passing on November 2, 2013, Governor Carroll was quoted as saying the following in the November 4, 2013 edition of *The Courier-Journal*: "Peter really became most interested in the department's programs because of his long-standing belief of taking care of people who can't take care of themselves."

Chapter 2

Relocating from Florida to Kentucky

In 2000, Peter and I were married and still working together at his thriving Miami-based business. Born in New York where he resided for his first couple of years, he grew up in Kentucky and considered this the place of his roots, the place where he left his signature. Peter had hoped to retire to his roots in Louisville, Kentucky, where we could live out our lives to the fullest. We enthusiastically agreed to work for the next several years and save our nest egg to buy a home and create a new life without the business. Six months before our planned move to Kentucky, we advertised our home for sale with two local real-estate agencies.

About the same time, Peter began showing the initial signs of Parkinson's disease in his right hand. Bewildered by the thought that Peter could have such an affliction, I learned later that he had researched the disease and knew it was true. I could not deny it any further. Soon after, he also began showing signs of memory problems.

While running errands one afternoon, as I was walking to my car, I caught a glimpse of the Alzheimer's Support Center, which gave me pause. I turned around and went into this center. I told the nurse about my husband and my concerns. I explained that, as the person closest to my husband, I wanted to gather information. I was also searching for a reliable local place for Peter to find firsthand knowledge and support. After repeatedly asking the staff if I could learn from them, they insisted they could not help me since I was not the patient. They were adamant that Peter needed to come in for testing. I told Peter about this incident, but he indicated that he did not want to pursue it further. I think I realized the importance of trying to do something upfront to help myself cope. As we accelerated our plans to leave Miami for a new life in Louisville, I was aware of the undeniable reality that Peter was experiencing more symptoms. Something was going horribly wrong; my concerns mounted.

In 2003, we made two trips to Louisville and contracted with Realtors there to search for a home for us. We visualized a home on spacious grounds with nature close by, one that would accommodate Peter's office and my art studio. Frustrated that we were unable to find something we liked on our first trip, we tried something else: an online search. After searching, we saw two listings that had every feature we wanted in our home and so close to what we had wished for; it was uncanny. Peter and I laughed. We did not believe there could be an online listing that met all of our specific design features. One listing in particular struck us as a strong possibility. After making many phone calls back and forth with the owners, we arranged to make this our first stop of our second trip.

As Peter was packing the car to leave on our second trip to Louisville, our neighbor Marc stopped to talk to him as he was walking his dog. Marc told Peter that he noticed our for-sale sign in the yard and was interested. He said he was temporarily renting a house down the street until he could buy a house on our street. He commented that he liked the location on Biscayne Bay Peninsula. He could dock his boat, watch the dolphins frolicking in the Bay waters, and walk his dog on a quiet street with little traffic. Peter told Marc that we were on our way to Louisville to look at houses where we intended to move and that he would get back to him when we returned. Marc gave Peter his business card. Peter came back into the house with bold enthusiasm about a business card he was holding in his hand. With such excitement, I could not imagine what was so important. He was just out in the driveway packing our suitcases into the car, and now this? With every bit of confidence in his voice, he explained, "We just found a buyer for our house!" He handed me the business card and said, "Keep this and let's call this guy when we get back." I thought to myself, *wow, now that is wishful thinking!*

Once we arrived in Louisville, we stopped to see the first of two houses we had found on the Internet. Even though our first house-hunting trip to Louisville was disappointing, we allowed ourselves to get excited as we drove down the driveway to the house we thought could be ours. After spending time with the owners and walking through the house, we were quite surprised to see everything we wanted in a home unfolding before our eyes. That night, we went to sleep on it. The next day, we made a decision to buy this house and make it our special place. As it turned out, this home was perfect for us and had the potential for any future renovations needed to accommodate us in our eventual twilight years.

Upon returning home, Peter reminded me to call our neighbor Marc. After seeing our house and after some consideration, Marc offered to buy it. Nothing could have felt better than moving into an experience that was harmonious with our desires to relocate — and we paid zero realtor fees at either end!

Before relocating to Louisville, our plan was to trade in Peter's two aging Volvos for a compact SUV, so we could travel to our new home in comfort. About two weeks before leaving Miami, we drove to a nearby auto dealership, purchased a new SUV, and drove it home. When I woke up the next morning, Peter was already in the driveway getting familiar with the instrument panel, which appeared highly complicated compared to the Volvo. Several hours later, he came into the house and expressed his anxiety and disappointment of having a very trying time becoming acquainted with the operation of this vehicle. I was surprised when he questioned his learning curve abilities. Since Peter was a licensed pilot, and, he was always on the cutting edge of computer use and technology, I had a hard time believing that this new vehicle could fluster him — but it did. Sadness and disappointment flashed through my mind. I wondered if I had just caught a glimpse of what lie ahead. I felt deeply for Peter, hugged him tightly and assured him that it was okay.

We decided to call off the idea of a new vehicle and went back to the dealership in the hopes of being able to exchange the new SUV for our two Volvos. Our salesperson refused to have compassion for Peter and our situation. He denied our request to honor the reversal of our agreement, and demanded that we pay a contract cancelation fee for breaking the agreement, which we did. We loaded one of our Volvos on the moving van, and Peter drove the other to our final destination.

Realizing the level of impairment of Peter's mental abilities at that time, I look back in bewilderment at his competent driving from Miami to Louisville, without incident. It was as though he had a mission, and he was destined to accomplish the next step in the realization of our dream. We were delighted to move into our new home by the end of September 2003.

Chapter 3

Coping with Peter's Diagnosis

Any hopes and dreams of continuing the vigorous life that Peter had lived were destined to fade into the powers of the choice of his soul. When I sensed the possibility of our future journey becoming a life about long-term illness, I felt stunned. Blindsided by the circumstances of our situation, I experienced an overwhelming loss of emotional stamina. I wondered how (and if) I could acclimate to this new life and still keep our connection to the deep love we shared. My immediate concern was my sense of helplessness. How could I be there for Peter? When your loved one faces serious illness, I feared that he was also wondering about coping with the loss of hope, understanding, and control. I realized that I needed first to take care of my mental and emotional self so that I have the capacity needed to support of my dear, wonderful husband. This sober reflection led me to appreciate, with gratitude, the significance of my vital role.

While Peter coped with feelings of hopelessness and anxiety about his illness, we found blissful distraction in the work of settling in our new home. My initial introduction to Kentucky quickly proved to be disappointing. I realized that Peter's health problems were turning our life around. It no longer resembled our initial dream of giving up the business in Miami to retire in Louisville, a place where

Peter planned to reacquaint himself with his roots and introduce me to a new experience. Although we believed the pull to relocate to Kentucky felt right, we also saw a vision clouded by images of other concerns that could suppress and overwhelm our dreams.

Because Peter's immediate family had moved to the D.C./Virginia area of the country, we had no relatives living in Kentucky. Peter had been living in Florida for twenty-five years before returning to his roots in Kentucky. Our efforts to reunite with his many friends, people he knew in politics statewide and his childhood did not materialize. His best friend and contact for state government employment, a woman who had vacationed with us in Miami a year before we moved to Louisville, had recently succumbed to illness before we could see her. Peter had hopes that public-sector work in local politics would offer meaningful challenges and an opportunity to perform socially important work once again, but that was not meant to be.

Shades of a different kind of life colored the landscape of each new day. With more clarity, eventually it became obvious to us that we were painting a portrait representing our new life, a painting that we began creating two years prior to leaving Miami. As we began embracing the vision of our new journey, my energies shifted to my dear husband and a situation that he could not control or make better. As our lives seemed to take on a new composition, I watched Peter struggle, and I tried to understand what it was like for him. As I observed a man of great integrity and perseverance, I could see the changed look in his eyes when he glanced at me — the look of uncertainty, of the courage to dream of things that were and never can be again.

Six months after moving to Louisville, we visited a neurologist, and Peter's diagnosis was Alzheimer's disease, until further testing.

Soon afterward, we learned of a holistic health care facility where Peter took treatments for several months in hopes of slowing the progress of his disease. When the treatments did not seem to change his condition appreciably, he tried the standard drug treatments available in 2004. Due to severe side effects and on the recommendation of his neurologist, Peter discontinued their use.

In 2004, I thought …*What can I do to nourish our inner freedom with vitality? What experiences might recapture some of Peter's best loved times growing up in Louisville? What hobbies, activities, or even just spending time embracing nature and music can we enjoy while Peter is still able to find joy in such pleasures?* I began to plan outings with activities that required a lot of Peter as long as he was still able.

High on the list was Peter's love of flying an airplane. The expansive arch of sunny skies over South Florida is where he found serenity, quietude, and lots of light. Years ago, Peter sold his airplane, so we rented an airplane at Bowman Airfield, the place where he studied and became a licensed pilot in 1984. During our visit, Peter enjoyed engaging in great conversations with the other pilots, reminiscing about the joy of flying. I took pleasure in observing how obvious it was that pilots have a very special connection and camaraderie. We all discussed Peter's illness and expressed disappointment that he would no longer be able to fly alone or with me. Feeling Peter's desire to experience his love of flying at least once more, the instructor suggested that Peter could fly, piloted by another aviator, which he did. Over the period of a year, we returned to the airfield and scheduled a few more flights, but I could tell that something was wrong. Cold feet and hesitation set in, and Peter seemed to lose his confidence and enthusiasm as the months passed. I watched him climb into the airplane and take off as I waited at the airfield. When the two returned very soon, the pilot explained that Peter seemed uncomfortable flying and insisted that they come back sooner than expected. A couple of months later, we scheduled another flight but Peter refused to get into the airplane.

After that, I read a list of items Peter had written down for himself, including a particularly heartbreaking decision for the both of us: "Give up flying." I was astonished when I saw those words, and I wept. I knew how much Peter loved flying for pleasure — it was the love of his life.

Peter struggled to continue to find an expression for his desire to make a difference in the lives of those experiencing his same illness. We sat down one day, and he began dictating his initial thoughts as I typed them out verbatim, as follows:

> "Careco (*the company name of Peter's business in Florida*) proposes establishing a program for worthy children, parents, and others who persistently face the terror and fear that pervades people of all ages living predominately with Alzheimer's disease. As previously announced, Careco will provide a number of services to children and adults. These services will join with other services provided by other services for children and youth. A number of these providers will lend assistance to predominantly local caregivers. Services will be provided by (list of names)."

Peter's ever-changing condition forced us to set aside his vision and noble effort to create programs to enrich others in his same situation. I did my best to reassure him that his love and sympathy for others counted for something. My love and admiration for him grew even deeper.

Peter was a perpetual student, and his interests spanned many fields encompassing his arresting knowledge. As a professional photographer in his college years, he loved to capture fascinating sights. When he was not working, he often had a camera on his shoulder or in his hands, photographing or video taping scenes wherever the moment caught his focus. In Miami, some of his favorite eye-catching spectacles were birds, animals, fish, plants; and especially vivid images of his pet gold and blue McCaw, named PJ, our pet iguana, Iggy and four feral cats. There were many magnificent rainbows and sunsets in their most significant beauty on Biscayne Bay that excited our esthetic pleasure with lingering looks — all in the name of capturing the essence of nature.

In Louisville, Peter photographed our first snowfall and ice storm in 2004, the water Hyacinth plants and Koi in our pond, and the strikingly colorful mallards wading in our creek. When birds began nest-building on the roof of our deck, he took pictures each day while scavenged materials were brought up to structure an exquisite nest. Mother bird dropping worms down the throats of her newborns and frame by frame, the fledglings' first flights were captured on film. Peter enjoyed the captivation of this enduring hobby longer than any other pastime.

A veteran of newspaper, magazine and broadcast journalism, and producer of hundreds of business plans and proposals, Peter's desire to write a children's book was *again* taking shape after many years of research. While looking forward to retirement, he revisited his longing to write a book based on one of his favorite children's fantasy novels that was out-of-print; *The Children's Country*, published in 1929 by Kay Burdekin.

Although Peter initially began researching the location of this book around 1974, it was not until 2002 that his diligent search verified that the book was possibly in Public Domain. At the University of Florida, he met with Professor John Cech, a well-known author of children's literature who also had an interest in this book. They discussed their desire to create a fresh, contemporary retelling of the original tale, and a possible film project.

Peter had a keen interest in movies, and he collected many of the films he was passionate about for home viewing. He studied the history of films and the backgrounds of his favorite actors. Shortly before relocating to Louisville, his interest in films led him to producing his first small film about the habits of a double-crested cormorant in the South Florida Everglades. Unfortunately, Peter's dream of pursuing this new hobby and writing a children's book with a possible film project, ran counter to other important times of our new life.

He enjoyed spending time surveying the celestial spheres and studying configurations of the stars, so this seemed like another area of interest that he could revisit with enthusiasm. And he did! We purchased a telescope, and our salesperson generously gave Peter instructions on its use. After Peter had spent some time and great effort recapturing the essence of his former hobby, we realized that it was lost, forever. We instead reminisced about the past when we held hands while sitting under the wide and starry sky after a long day at work in Miami. Embraced by the warm breezes of hot summer evenings while gazing, Peter delineated the configurations. We still have these memories, and I know that he is worth so much more than the things he left behind. For this, I am grateful.

Naturally drawn to water sports throughout his life, Peter was an avid scuba diver, underwater photographer, and swimmer who loved to sail and spend time on his boat. Since we no longer lived in a tropical climate, year-round water sports became a seasonal indulgence. Until spring arrived, we joined our local fitness club to swim and exercise. After observing the pool, Peter gave his halfhearted support, and there was no convincing him to enjoy the sensation of swimming.

Against Peter's wishes to try something new, I persuaded him to take dance classes to exercise his limbs and focus his attention. At home, we practiced his dance steps by drawing diagrams on large pieces of white paper and placing them on the floor to show him where to place his feet. It was so hilarious that we laughed until our sides hurt. Peter made an earnest attempt to do something he would never have chosen to do if it were not for my asking. Although our dance lessons were short-lived, it was worth the try. In my heart, a spark of gratefulness lives on for the fun we had together. I cannot help "smiling out loud" every time I think about it.

Peter and I enjoyed spending time outdoors at our home, the sanctuary where I could always observe his calm repose and feel his sweet, gentleness. We had wonderful memories of hiking and sightseeing at the tropical parks in Florida, so we began visiting many of the great, quiet parks and lakes in Louisville. There, we filled ourselves with the splendor of mingling with our creative force of nature. When moving around became more difficult for Peter, we hired a minivan and driver to take us to our favorite places. We were able to experience the cooling shade of the graceful trees, the sweet fragrance of the flowers and the boundless life of the small creatures of the Earth. Thanks, for the strength and relief, we were then able to greet serenely and bow to our other challenges. These gracious and inspiring surroundings reassured us that there was still beauty and hope in our lives. Lively and abundant, these memories will always leave their mark on me.

In those too-frequent times when too many things got in the way, we always found support and inspiration in listening to our favorite operas, such as Turandot and Madama Butterfly. We enjoyed classical music and artists, such as Sarah Brightman, Kiri Te Kanawa, Pavarotti, among many, many others. We paid particular attention to our quietude as our life's emphasis undeniably changed from *tangible* to more *intangible* pursuits.

Chapter 4

Tara Reaches for Emotional Support

My husband and I had always made our most important decisions together. As his abilities began to crumble, the increasing burden of once-shared responsibilities began to fall heavily on my shoulders alone. It weighed on my emotional upheaval that had already set in, and at times, our plans seemed to fall apart. I found myself saddened, disappointed and depressed. This was normally not a part of my personality, but I felt so overwhelmed and discouraged. I was unfamiliar with my surroundings and had no support system in place. Dreary clouds sometimes cast a thick gloom over our days. I could not quiet the song in my heart for the love I had for Peter, but at the same time, his unbearable condition tugged on my heart. I wondered how he could endure his ill health.

With only a few friends in the Louisville area, I felt an overpowering loneliness. The only support I could get from those closest to us during long distant telephone calls was, "Oh, things will get better!" While sobbing and crying, I would hang up the telephone and feel myself slipping deeper into despair. No one realized what Peter and I were coping with and how distraught and devastated I felt, or that I was desperately reaching out for help. The small family support group we did enjoy was too far away to fuel our needs for the close, personal love and energy we needed on a continual basis.

I wondered where I could go for help and how I should handle this dilemma. Eventually, I sought counseling to strengthen my reserve and embrace my challenging role to ensure that Peter knew that I would always love him and take care of him. In my confusion, I began making phone calls in an effort to make connections with a respected counselor. When the phone book did not yield an answer, I remembered that Peter's mother once mentioned how she loved to take young Peter to the Jewish Family Community Services Center to swim. With trepidation, I located the center. I walked across the parking lot drawn to the sound of splashing water and children's voices bursting with laughter. I spotted a large swimming pool and felt a sigh of relief as I approached the fence surrounding the pool area. I gazed eagerly at the little children swimming with excitement and having fun. I remember feeling lighter, with a sense of happiness and serenity. I stopped to pretend, just for that moment, that I was visualizing Peter's mother smiling and watching Peter as a child playing in the pool, swimming joyfully. I realized that when pausing and reflecting, light penetrates a gnawing darkness. I felt that I was in the right place and perhaps I could find help here. As I walked over to the counselor's office, I was welcomed.

The counselor and I talked about how frightened I was, and I shared that I was slowly losing my strength and courage to cope. I loved my husband deeply and did not want him to feel that he was losing me. As far back as I could remember, I was a tower of strength and always capable of coping on my own, but this experience was somehow different. This time, I had another person's life in the balance. I envisioned the day when I could no longer leave Peter alone for he would need someone with him at all times. There's nothing like something coming at you that's not going to stop.

Reaching out for this kind of help was in my best interest at this time. I did not know what to expect, but after a few visits, just sitting and talking about this new life that Peter and I embraced, my coping skills seemed to improve. I began taking Peter to our meetings so that the counselor could assess our situation more fully. Peter and I felt joyful knowing that we were doing something together, spending quality time, and for a good reason. My faith in our efforts to share this life-changing circumstance mitigated my pain.

After the counselor and I had discussed how my lack of proper rest was adversely influencing my ability to attend to Peter's needs, she suggested a bold new idea. At her urging, I began searching for an adult daycare center for Peter to spend a few hours a day, a few days per week. She and I felt that doing so would benefit us both greatly. I would have some time alone to restore my inner strength, and Peter would have a different environment to play in. Peter was not very keen on the idea, but at the same time, I did not know of an alternative. I needed a break from the stress. I spent a great deal of time visiting different adult daycare centers until I found one that could be an enjoyable experience for him. After enrolling, he went along and tried to participate in the activities and physical exercises. The only thing Peter wanted to do was stand at the podium where the activities director spoke to the group. So much of his life had evolved around public speaking, and that is where he felt most comfortable.

After a few months of visits with the counselor, I was feeling stronger, but Peter began objecting to spending time at the adult daycare center. Once we arrived at daycare, he wanted to stay in the car with me. Most days, he asked if he could go with me instead. I did not like the situation either; I wanted us to be together too. I tried to explain that I needed time for rest and reflection in order to balance our responsibilities. Most importantly, I reassured Peter that I wanted to promote a healthy environment filled with love and spiritual aliveness for the both of us. Nevertheless, as soon as I started to leave the daycare center, Peter attempted to leave with me. Even explaining to him that this was for me, and it was something I needed so that we could spend the rest of the day together, he was not willing. He was not interested in socializing with the others; he did not fit in with the group situation. Once resigned to the idea that I was going to be away for a while, he went directly to the nurse's office and slept until I returned to him.

Soon, Peter began having problems with his balance. It was not safe to continue leaving him in the hands of others who did not know him as well as I did, so we stopped going to the daycare. I understood why this situation was not the most ideal for someone like Peter, a leader who was always in charge of his life. While the arrangement did provide the needed benefit of my self-help, daycare was not the optimal choice for my dear, wonderful husband.

We contemplated other possibilities. So that I could take some time out for myself and Peter could stay at home, we hired a companion to stay with him a few hours a day. At last, Peter was very happy with this arrangement, as was I. Years later we enlisted professional caregivers on a daily basis. When Peter's condition became more severe, and additional assistance was needed, we engaged our local medical house-call provider, MD2U to perform procedures normally carried out at a doctor's office or medical facility. Doctors and nurses came to our home on a regular basis to perform basic monitoring and exams. Eventually, I learned how to operate the equipment to administer medications and fluids intravenously myself.

At times, especially when we went out to lunch and dinner dates, Peter made our life rather lively. As soon as we sat down at our table, he would leave and visit other people in the restaurant, introducing his self and shaking hands with as many people as he could. I understood that as a former public official, handshakes and introductions were the natural things to do. Although I was amused but astonished at the same time, my need to leave my seat repeatedly to coax Peter back to our table diverted our attention from enjoying the dining experience. Sometimes, after leaving the restaurant, we would drive home, prepare a meal, and eat in our kitchen because we were still hungry. We experienced many uncommon moments such as this; with a great deal of patience and understanding on my part, they would guarantee laughter and lighten up the seriousness of our situation. I am still so happy that Peter has left these memories for me to dwell upon. In these moments, I can open myself up to some of the joy of our lives together.

Later on, our counselor further suggested that I begin attending group, caregiver support meetings. I agreed that this would be helpful, and I enjoyed meeting others in my same situation. Although I was away for only a short time, I always missed my husband and hurried back home to join him. Our desire to be close did not change; I wanted to share a life with Peter and be there to love and support him.

Throughout the years, while others continually suggested that I needed to do something more for myself, that advice never resonated with me. It caused me to ignore their concerns, even as I also appreciated them. When I felt it was necessary, I carved out time for myself to do sculpting and take electronic keyboard classes to balance my time with Peter. I think you have to know yourself underneath. Because I believed our journey had a much greater purpose that I did not quite understand yet, I chose to follow my heart. I sometimes pondered what else was possible for us as long as I was in alignment with my heart and soul.

As time passed, we felt even closer. Peter and I are soul mates. We were best friends, and Peter was the love of my life. He always let me be myself, and never judged me. I forever felt I could reside in his love and just be me. When you are taking care of a loved one, someone you do not want to lose, you become closer and more attuned to each other. You feel more deeply loved by one another — and so it was with us.

Chapter 5

Unexpected Challenges

Looking at our situation with new eyes, I threw myself even more passionately into Peter's care. I was determined to do whatever it took so that we could stay together in our home, regardless of the new challenges. My commitment to maintaining Peter's dignity far outweighed any new difficulties we might face. Confronted with new and daring changes over the next seven years, in spite of their opposition, no matter what life asked of us, our new life presented us with opportunities for learning, and many gifts of joy and happiness, as well.

In spite of his illness, Peter had a very pleasant disposition. He reveled in taking advantage of situations open for an opportunity to provoke laughter with his keen sense of wit and humor. He had a gift for shedding light on meaningless and irrational situations.

Peter always took pleasure in driving, but he grew less capable behind the wheel, and it frightened me. I did my best to convince him to let me do all the driving, but knowing that his driving privileges were in jeopardy, he resisted the inevitable. We had been going together for chiropractic treatments for about a month, and against Peter's wishes, I drove. One particular day, as we prepared to visit the chiropractor's office, Peter gave me a real scare. I called for him, but he did not answer. He was nowhere in the house. The last place

I checked was the garage, and when I opened the door to the garage, my heart sank. I could not believe my eyes; the car was missing, and so was Peter! He had driven off. Out of a deep concern for his safety and for that of others, I called the police station and reported my distressful situation. I could hardly control my emotions.

A police officer came to the house, and we filled out a report. In that effort, I felt a temporary relief, but that vanished as quickly as it came over me when the officer left. How could I possibly get Peter back? Where else should I call? I was emotionally distraught and could only cry. We had a second car, so I decided to drive around the neighborhood, searching for clues to where he could have driven. It was hopeless, and there was no sign of him, so I returned home and thought about what to do next. Since Peter knew we had an appointment to see the chiropractor, I called the doctor's office and explained my situation. I asked that they immediately call me if Peter showed up. I did not believe that he could have driven that far because it was a very long distance, and the directions were a little complicated. Although we had made this trip many times before, and I drove, it was hard for me to believe that Peter would have remembered how to get there and back home on his own. I was fighting a mental battle, and I had nowhere to turn. When mired in the emotions of how all of this is taking place, it is difficult to see the reality of your issues.

Under a surge of distressing emotions, I decided to drive to the doctor's office and see if I could find Peter. I drove around and drove around with no clues. I parked the car and went in the doctor's office, but once I learned that Peter had not been there, I left, distraught. On my way home, I clung desperately to the hope that Peter was already home, but he was not. I cried more and called the police station again. The police had no clues after searching the area around our home.

Approximately four hours later, I heard the automatic garage door open. I ran into the kitchen, opened the door to the garage, and saw Peter very slowly driving into the garage, unscathed. As emotionally distraught as I had been for the past four hours, I still cried with palpable emotions when I saw him in the car. I hurried over to him before he could get out of the car and prepared myself to hold him close. As he stepped outside of the car, we stood together and hugged each other. In his imposing frame and embrace, I began to find calm again. I always found refuge in his arms. As I dried my tears, and we walked into the house, I asked him where he had been. He did not know. Then I asked him if he had stopped anywhere, maybe at a restaurant since he was missing for so long. He told me he visited a pet hospital where the staff invited him in to use their bathroom. Once I remembered that there *was* an animal hospital next door to the doctor's office, I wondered to myself if Peter had driven to the doctor's office and back home on his own.

After having time to think about what had happened, I realized that Peter's solo adventure was a product of fear and his determination not to lose the right to drive. In his struggle, I learned about what he was experiencing. How he fought against the loss of being independent, the loss of the abilities that once defined him, and the loss of control revealed so much to me. Peter had to show his will in the face of a real disagreement. He faced an enormous challenge to find the courage to let go and give those rights over to me.

In September 2005, Peter received an invitation to speak about his illness to an Alzheimer's Foundation support group. He was very eager to oblige and prepared by gathering his thoughts and dictating them to me as I wrote them down verbatim. Together, we created the script for his presentation. When we arrived at the group setting, Peter was beaming with enthusiasm. Knowing how much he enjoyed speaking in public, I was delighted to see his sense of control and confidence.

At the same time, I secretly felt torn by *my* emotions as I slipped into a state of powerless control. Although I was not a public speaker, I was stunned by a part of me that was visualizing *myself* speaking to this group and carrying an enormous amount of anxiety and self-doubt about coping with my imagined performance in front of a group. Blinded by this veil of anxiety clouding my vision, I felt paralyzed with overwhelming apprehension and fear; I could not see clearly or move my body in the chair I was sitting on! Then I thought, if this did not fit my situation, perhaps I was bursting with anguish from pent-up emotions and the pressures of responsibilities that I was dealing with that day and for the past two years. I wanted Peter's experience to be very special for us, but the effort to keep my composure in the face of his courage was a lot to bear. As Peter stepped up to the podium, my fright gradually dissipated. I realized that Peter did *not* need *me; I* needed Peter.

I had the privilege to see him speak his truth with the most beautiful mental and moral courage. This is what he said:

> "Good morning. My name is Peter Conn, and I have Alzheimer's disease. I'm here to share some of my experiences over the last year and a half since my diagnosis. My background in newspapers and government has always put me in front of an audience. My family-owned newspapers here, *The Jefferson Reporter* and I grew up writing and editing before going into state government. I served two terms in the Kentucky Legislature and was Secretary of Human Resources during the Julian Carroll administration

in 1977. For the last twenty-five years, I owned and operated a consulting firm in Florida, writing business plans and proposals. My wife, Tara, joined me during the last thirteen years of a very successful business. We moved back to my Kentucky roots two years ago.

Now with Alzheimer's. My wife Tara helps me to shower and shave. She picks out my clothes and assists me in any way she can each day.

I'm a pilot, but I can only be airborne with another pilot assisting me.

Driving my car is one of the pleasures I miss most. My wife does all the driving now.

Finishing sentences is sometimes a nightmare. I feel so frustrated at times, but at other times, I have no problem getting my thoughts across.

My energy and drive to do things wanes, sometimes.

I feel down and unhappy at times because my life has changed so much. In spite of it, I'm very fortunate to have a wonderful wife and home life that I wouldn't trade for anything. I am thankful for the life that I have for there are many others that are far worse off than I am. And that's why I'm here today, to share my experiences, past, and present, and hope that I am still able to make a difference in others' lives. Thank you for inviting me."

Peter's willingness and determination to express his self before a group and talk about his illness to those in his same situation was truly revealing and supportive of those listening. His performance was outstanding, but sadly, this was the last time he spoke before a group.

When Peter's ability to communicate progressively waned, he became very frustrated. I clearly recall a time early on when Peter made a strenuous effort to communicate with me about something very important to him. When I asked him to tell me what it was, he said, "Will you get me my case?" I was a little puzzled as to why he would ask me for his case, so I asked him several times again to repeat it. I got the same response. I brought to him a few of his cases — briefcases, eyeglass cases, camera cases, travel cases of all sorts. I even brought him a pillowcase, only to see a disappointing look on his face. Caring deeply and knowing that I was the only one he could rely upon, it troubled me that I did not know what he wanted.

During the next ten days, before going to sleep I prayed aloud so that Peter could hear me. I called upon the highest powers of the universe and asked, "How can I find Peter's case?" Finally, I received an answer that came to me in my dream state. I envisioned a gray, lightweight sweater cap that he always wore to keep his head warm. When I showed him, he smiled broadly, I smiled back, and then I woke up from my dream. It was amazing! I felt compelled to see if that was what Peter wanted, so I flew out of bed, ran down the hall to the closet, and picked out a few caps and hats from his collection. When Peter woke up, I showed him what I had in my hands and asked him if this was what he wanted. As I put one of the caps on his head, he looked up at me wide-eyed and smiled sweetly. My eyes filled with tears of joy, for I *knew* that his cap/hat was what he wanted. At that moment, I realized just how something that small has such big meaning and importance. He had beautiful, dark hair and a lot of it — until he started losing it on the top of his head. That is when wearing these caps to keep his head warm came into style. I thought to myself, *Well, the word 'case' starts with c a, and 'cap' starts with c a, so that made sense.*

For the first couple years spent in Louisville, we saw many different doctors and tried various treatments to slow the progression of Peter's disease. At the same time, we filled our precious time together indulging in enjoyable activities when we needed play time. Despite Peter's challenge to maintain his balance and my efforts to keep him from straying, we went to the theaters and movies, we went bowling and to the zoo, and we visited a few friends. On pleasant days, we took monthly day trips to the parks and lakes to feed the ducks and other birds, or explored the mall to escape the rain or cold.

In August 2006, we sought more insight on Peter's condition from another neurologist and received a complete evaluation. After undergoing a neuropsychological evaluation that more fully pinpointed significant impairment of his orientation and verbal skills, his diagnosis was Lewy Body Dementia and Parkinsonism. The doctor began by asking Peter, "Do you know why you are here?" Peter quipped, "If I knew, I wouldn't be here!" We all laughed as I reminded myself of how he could always amuse me with his sense of humor. I thought about how important laughter is when dealing with serious matters.

Peter began in-home physical therapy, followed by two years of therapy at a rehabilitation center twice a week for gait and balance training. In 2007, we purchased a Parkinson walker. We hired a masseuse and purchased a massage table for home use so that Peter did not have to miss his weekly massage. We then bought an oversized recliner so that we could sit together while reading and drawing.

In 2008, after trying various wheelchairs that were incompatible with Peter's height, we purchased a custom designed tilt-back wheelchair. And when Peter could no longer bear his weight, we used a Capella lift to move him from place to place. In 2009, we ordered a remote-controlled stair lift so that Peter could navigate the stairs. Installed on his birthday, as Peter waited at the top of the stairs for his gift, the minute he saw the stair lift operating, he happily exclaimed, "hot *dog!*" And so the stair lift was named.

When Peter's neck and head needed extra support, his doctor fitted him for a collar. We had an ankle/calf support molded to fit his left lower leg when his foot became weak and rotated inward. Knowing that Peter needed help to do almost everything, my dream was to ensure that his bathing habits continued on a near-normal basis too. We remodeled the shower stall and purchased a specially designed shower chair to enable Peter to move freely in and out of our bathroom facility.

Peter's physical abilities continued to decline, and he began to lose his ability to speak fluently. Words no longer came easily, and when I asked him to describe what it was like, he said, "It feels like I have blanks in my mind." He struggled with great dignity when no one else who knew him saw how brave and courageous he was in the face of failing health. Sometimes the words just came out a little different, but I *usually* knew what he meant. There were times when Peter spoke someone's name a little dissimilar, such as when he addressed my sister Suzanne, as "SuAna," the endearing name that she continues to use.

Because Peter was no longer experiencing appreciable improvement, his physical therapist determined that therapy was insufficient for his needs. Instead, we used a massage vibrator for the circulation of his feet and legs, and our caregivers and I did physical therapy for his body each morning. Around 2010, the stair lift became a safety issue when Peter could no longer hold his body in an upright posture, even with the assistance of additional belts to secure him. That's when we said bye-bye to Hot Dog and hello to an elevator, enabling Peter to move with ease upstairs, downstairs, and outside in his wheelchair.

My heart always knew the value of maintaining Peter's integrity and supporting him with compassion and gentleness every step of the way. I never felt I was *sacrificing* anything; I considered this a part of shaping our journey. When I thought about how Peter struggled to make his every move assisted by another, how could I *ever* entertain the thought that I was sacrificing *my* life. Dark days transformed into amazingly joyful serenity with a gaze into Peter's eyes, the place where I saw the emotions he held deeply. No one could ever put a spark in my eyes the way he did.

In this momentary space, I reminisce about our experiences in this vast gulf of emotions, humbled by the comparison between what I write here and now, and how Peter was before his illness. I wish I could articulate the disparity between the depth of his downfallen path and the intensity and beauty of his unceasing courage and dignity. My love and admiration for Peter runs deep, and he still moves me inexpressively. Although our story eventually reveals a grand and unexpected outcome, these present thoughts and sensations wring tears out of me as I write this. In the hope of offering support to those in similar situations, let me simply say this: *Find comfort in your time with your loved one. Give as much love, respect, and validation as you possibly can. This type of illness is ambiguous, and your loved one gradually changes. Regardless of your many defeated hopes, being in the higher energies in a loving soul-to-soul connection on those special moments — when they happen — is magical.*

Chapter 6

Finding a New Way to Communicate with Peter

As I repeatedly redefined our lives, I searched for solutions that would allow Peter and me to continue living together in our home. We worked diligently to attain a level of understanding of what the meaning of our journey meant. We sought to attain a new awareness that our experience may have a grand effect on the material and non-material worlds in which we lived. As the years passed and we overcame each new challenge, I realized that this is a life through illness and beyond — a spiritual as well as a physical journey for both of us. We realized that we were part of something very different, something bigger than we could totally grasp for ourselves. This knowledge nurtured and supported us throughout the years. I remember some of the last words Peter spoke to me. Among the many reminders of his love for me, he reminded me: "take care of yourself" and "always stay sweet and beautiful." It was so heartbreaking to hear those words come out of his mouth. As I stood there, engulfed in a tide of emotions, I asked myself if this was an urgent message from his soul, expressing an intended good-bye. I was unprepared for that message.

Approximately six years before his passing, Peter had little to no ability to move his body or speak fluently. He spoke few to no words and eventually had no verbal skills. Even though after more than sixteen years together at this point, I was able to read his thoughts intuitively to a degree, it was far from an optimal way to communicate. Things seemed to be changing; Peter seemed to be changing. Peter had been exhibiting signs of despondency. He was not the same contented, sweet man I had always enjoyed. He also was not showing signs of affection toward me, and it was difficult for me to understand what was happening. Although I believed it was improbable, I *wondered* if he still loved me. I was feeling that he *minded* me assisting him. I kept asking myself if what I was doing was helping or harming him. I thought that perhaps a change in routine would be helpful to both of us to create a balance between reflection, quiet time, and involvement in the physical world. However, at the time, it seemed that I was doing everything to assist him, which was necessary for the sustenance of his life.

From that point on, any spiritual guidance I needed to support our journey became an inner search and healing process. At the outset, each time I came to Peter with love and concern, I looked at him in wonder. My judgments prevented me from seeing the truth in his eyes, and I became blinded by the brightness of his inner light. Somehow, Peter inspired me to find a way to impact the spiritual consciousness around me. Seeing beyond his appearance invoked in me a sense of finding out what was underneath.

Awakening to the challenge of suddenly having a *knowingness* that I can communicate with my loved one on a level beyond the everyday existence was a revelation. It was like surrendering to the unknown. Knowing that my higher self is always there to support and guide me, I now took intense pleasure in the deeper meanings of life, and, why we are here. The love and compassion we felt for each other allowed me to surrender to this new experience resonating inside me. I knew that when you are here in the body, anything is possible, and you can experience any level of that.

For many months, while falling asleep each night, I again prayed aloud so that Peter could hear me. I asked the highest powers of the universe for guidance to show me a way to reach him and know what he is thinking. As time clicked by, my efforts continued to compel me to discover a new way of communicating, from our hearts. I felt guided.

Shortly after and during a casual phone conversation with Beverly, Peter's former massage therapist and our dear friend in Miami, I learned about channeling our thoughts and heartfelt emotions on a higher plane. In spite of the fact that Peter was a self-proclaimed atheist who may not be open to exploring this idea, I continued to believe in the pursuit of my endeavor. Channeling eventually opened us up to view the inspired revelation of truths beyond the range of our ordinary human vision, a gift that is immeasurable. We consciously chose to identify with a direct connection to the divine, and the spiritual ideal to which we were committed existed out of the call of our souls. Perhaps Peter's disabilities were a disguised blessing.

Harking back to the personal intimacy of our many encounters with divine communications through channeling, I realized how Peter's astute words, spoken from his higher self, broadcast our truth. They spoke to the heart and soul of who we are as spiritual beings and why we came here. The love we shared during our spiritual journey of divine commitment continues to sustain me.

In 2011, during our initial channeling session with Sally Baldwin, our first channel medium, I discovered that Peter was encountering his higher self. He was relinquishing his human self — the body, mind and ego. He elevated himself through spiritual self-exploration and eventually relinquished any resistance to his limitations of physical immobility and the inability to speak. While I recognized our need to be physical and participatory in the material sense, Peter taught me the importance of being aware of our divine connection to the divine and beings that are ungrounded and subject to all the physical material things. Honoring each other in a soul-to-soul connection became our way of seeing each other as souls unattached to physical limitations or negative emotions. Soul-based communication became a beautiful, energetic exchange of loving support.

Chapter 7

Introduction to Channeled Transcriptions
(*Before* Peter's Transition on November 2, 2013)

I wish to start this chapter with a beautiful thought. *Wouldn't it be great if everyone who desired to do so could communicate with their loved ones, soul-to-soul, and know each other on a much deeper level?* With Peter and me, it was a spectacular reality. We realized our grand journey could serve as inspiration to others for a life in the highest vision, and at the same time honor our legacy. Not only did we know our experience meant grand revelations for us, but also it needed to bring gifts through and into the world for others. It is our hope that the transparency of our very personal and intimate experiences will enlighten others with the gift of spirituality and awareness that we are more than our physical bodies. It's time to open up to our loved ones in spirit and soul-to-soul communication.

The meaning of our revelations is essentially wordless. The experience breaks past the words, so let us take our energies and have an incredibly beautiful and divine dance in the energetic field. Everyone can learn to experience an extraordinary range of human spiritual life by dancing in the energetic field with their loved ones. There is a message in this for seekers who are willing to welcome our story about a deeper meaning of communicating soul-to-soul. The spiritual potentialities of all of us are there, waiting to be born.

The magic of the outcome of our journey reveals itself through the courtesy of recorded channeled transcriptions of our communications, which began in 2011, nearly three years *after* Peter lost his human voice and the ability to move his body. Up until then, we lived day after day with thanks pouring out of our hearts that we were still here together as months turned into years. On our little isle of life, we found the courage to jump to a higher resting place where the song in our hearts could be heard, and our emotions could be felt. Peter wanted me to know what his soul was experiencing. I wanted to learn the meaning of expanding my spiritual awareness so I could embrace our true potential as spiritual beings. This great blessing of communing soul-to-soul intertwined in our decade-long journey speaks to the truth of who we are and what we came here to do.

Our journey is not just about channeling; it is about an experience that is much grander, much more expansive than that. It is about learning how to share the wisdom and power of communing through life soul-to-soul, regardless of whether the soul is in the physical or spiritual realm. You will fully engage in the spiritual experience of Peter's journey evolving from a place of illness through his transition into the spirit world and beyond. It was never just about us figuring it out and then allowing ourselves to benefit from it. Both of us have always felt that what we benefit from we want to share in this world. We want to give to others so that they can then feel what we felt (and still feel). We were (and still are) blessed and honored to be so gifted through our experience in this world.

The intention of these discourses is to bring about the sound spiritual awareness that we are first spiritual beings living in a human body, not human bodies with spirits. It is our divine right to exist in a manner that supports our souls, and it does not matter whether we are in a human body or spirit form. The following channeled transcriptions give Peter a voice during the time he was unable to speak in his human form. These gifts of knowledge are from direct communications with Peter's soul. His soul expressed the desire and willingness to share this experience so that our profound lessons could bring greater understanding of who we are. For those searching for a higher level of spiritual awareness, these gifts will be a bridge so that they too may feel entitled to have this kind of exchange.

Although our channeled conversations may seem daunting and improbable at first, for those willing to embrace our story, they have the power to stir your spirit and enlighten you. Peter's soul brings to light the spiritual side of us that is always present and there for us to tap into for its rewards. Regardless of any long-held beliefs about the mysteries of the spirit world, his soul speaks to the wisdom of how one can expand the knowledge of soul-to-soul communication by merging the spirit and physicality.

NOTES: We suggest that the following channeled transcriptions, which have been recorded and <u>transcribed verbatim,</u> are to be read in consecutive chapter order for continuity.

All wording in boldface type is the voice of *the soul of Peter D. Conn.* Other channeled conversations, for example, with "Lewis," are not in boldface type. However, they too have been recorded and <u>transcribed verbatim.</u>

Appearing in italics, portions within the transcriptions indicate paraphrasing of comments/short conversations by the writer and channel/medium. These portions serve to inform the reader and are valuable for the continuity of subsequent paragraphs.

You never know where your soul will take you.

Chapter 8

First Exchange in Nearly Three Years
Transcript of August 22, 2011
Channeled by Sally Baldwin, Channel/Medium

Tara expresses gratitude for this wonderful opportunity to reach Peter through a new level of communication. She familiarizes Sally with the circumstances of the past eight years, and more specifically, that Peter has been enduring the loss of his verbal skills and the inability to move his body for almost three years now. She explains how their situation has created a challenging lifestyle, inviting great hardship and emotional pain, especially and most profoundly for her dear, wonderful husband. She informs Sally that the onset of Peter's illness began in 2002 when he was fifty-nine years old.

Tara continues that she has been taking care of Peter in their home, along with other caregiving support, but it is difficult knowing if she is meeting Peter's needs on physical, emotional and spiritual levels. She wishes to bring about more understanding of her role as wife and caregiver. She believes that having a way of verbally communicating with Peter could be the key to not only assisting him more fully, but giving her a deeper connection to what is going on, and perhaps alleviating some of the emotional and physical challenges they face daily.

Tara: I am concerned about the shift I see in Peter's disposition, and that he seems despondent and unable to show affection toward me. I want to ask Peter if he still loves me. I also want to know if he is unhappy with the way I am taking care of him. Sally, please know that Peter is a very gentle soul and that I love him deeply. If you knew Peter previous to the onset of his illness, you would find it highly improbable to believe that he is in a body but has no way of expressing his self; it must be immensely unnerving.

Sally: Let's talk to him. Okay, Peter, come on in. Here is your moment.

Peter: I am the Peter you know and love, and who knows and loves you, and I am a bit insulted at this level that you would even question whether I love you, my dear. That needs to be pushed aside, and stop looking at yourself as if you haven't done enough for me. I'm not waiting for you to *do* anything for me. Just you being around and knowing you live under this roof with me is enough. In fact, *you doing* so much of it actually makes me feel a bit embarrassed as if I am somehow making you go way beyond the call of duty just so I receive something here. I have no way, of course, of making my wishes known or being able to let it out! But *I am here!* At this moment, in this particular juncture of my life, I'm so grateful that you found me this way, so that I *can* have this open, honest conversation with you, where I can tell you: *Stop giving* so much to me.

It is a feeling inside of me that is feeling despondent that you are not able to live your own life. I don't *want* to see you here always at my beck and call. I want you to be able to live your life

and to feel the *excitement* of it with the vibrancy that *you have* that I don't. Now do I *enjoy* whenever you are there? Do I *love* that you are around and that the touch is there and that energy that transmits between us? *Of course I do.* But it is not *enough* for me to just say, *I have* everything of my beloved Tara's attention. I want to be able to know that you take your *eyes* off me some so that I can take *my* eyes off *you* some. And so that each of us then can *find* where we belong and where we are.

I can't even answer your question honestly or truthfully because I don't know. I don't get enough time, enough energy, enough opportunity to feel where it is the other realms are and how I can traverse there. I feel as if everything is about coming right back into the body and paying attention *here* in the material world. I need, just as *you* need, a diversion of energy that says … we are not locked into each other as if there is some sort of *embalming* situation going on here that won't let the other one find their path. So you and I do each other the *best* favor when you can take your eyes off me, and let me develop whatever it is my connection with the other side can be at this moment — so I become more used to, more comfortable, more familiar and thus able to *let go* when that moment crosses for me.

I don't *do* that because I feel in some way that you don't have enough to do. You don't have a focus; you don't have a life other than me. So I *don't* want to leave you hanging. I don't want you left in some suspended empty void wondering what do I get up for every day. I want you to be able to say, "Look what I did today, Peter. Look what I'm all about. I feel so excited about this, about that, about what I've been involved in." I want you to stop making *me* your purpose. I want you to start living it from within and let me do the same, and then I *can* develop my pathway to another realm. Then I can explore it more and find a way to get there. And you and I will be both doing it with that open, loving, wondrous liberation that two souls who feel so entwined and so dear to each other can feel. That's what I want, and that's what I want for you.

Sally: Wow! That was great! Very good, Peter. Yeah, he *is* very gentle. He's a very gentle soul.

Tara: I wonder why Peter became ill. I guess you can't ask …

Sally: Oh, but *he* can tell us! Let's *ask* him. So this was so early, Peter, your onset of this. What's the deal?

Peter: Wish I had a clear-cut answer that I could tell you because I don't. But, I will say this; that I was willing in this life to take on an experience that would say:

> **"You know, as much as you loved and enjoyed and were enthralled with being a part of life in every way you could, you really were awful material about it, Peter. All you ever did was give yourself all the rational reasons for why you thought what you thought, saw what you saw, did what you did … and that *you didn't look deeper.*"**

This is an opportunity for me to take to my very heart and soul to say:

> **"*Look what this experience brought you?* … where you actually had to start letting go of the tethers of functioning in the normal material way. What did you learn from that? What is it that you're going to take with you as a soul that you'll recognize and know never leaves you?"**

You have no idea, my dear, beautiful Tara, how this affects me as an eternal being. I never have to have a life again where I'll step into such dysfunction and non-communicability, where I can actually take the energy of who I really am, and live it without having to go to such extremes. I was so caught up in the material, believing *that* was what everything was about and what it meant, that I didn't give enough credit or *depth* or exploring of that which is underneath it all. So this experience *made* me, *told* me:

> **"See, there's a whole other level of life, and when you're here in the body, anything is possible, and you can experience *any* level of that."**

Well, now I *know* it. So every bit of this, *every moment* of these years where it's been so painful, difficult, and hard to watch me kind of deteriorate, it has been on the other side an unbelievably *exalting* experience where it's helped me get to a place not of pride, but of humility and a sense of knowing there is a lot more to life than you think when you're running around functional and fully awake. So I *love* this, even as much as my physicality goes through it and has the hard struggle of it. I *love* it, and I'm *grateful* and have no regrets.

Tara: Oh wow, I need to step back and take a deep breath here. I'm stunned. I could not have known ...

[Pause here.]

Sally: So it's all good. That's the way you've got to think about it now, Tara, which will help you to take this next step you've got to take. Now you have a whole, deeper, and more full picture of what's really going on, and you have to start doing more of the spiritual and deeper choices.

So, Tara, there may be something in this journey here, especially with Peter, that you would do well to put to paper.

Tara: Oh … but *Peter* is the writer.

Sally: Well, that doesn't mean you're not too!

Tara: I … but I don't think that I can sit down and write like Peter! That was his whole life.

Sally: But no one's saying to write like Peter, it's write like Tara! You know, maybe one of the reasons he's still here is to see you get going on this. I mean, he hasn't been able to tell his story of these last few years, but *you* can! You know … so, that's something I would contemplate, and I would certainly be thinking about that if I were you.

Tara: Thank you, Sally. This has been an amazing experience!

Sally: Yes. You deserve it.

Tara: Thank you, Peter. I'm so grateful … I need to let all this settle in. I love you dearly.

[End of session/tape.]

Chapter 9

Second Exchange

Transcript of October 13, 2011
Channeled by Sally Baldwin, Channel/Medium

Tara: It has been so difficult to take in all of Peter's feelings and emotions during our first channeled session on August 22, 2011. I feel entangled in so many different emotions and responsibilities. Most of all, my heart carries a different perspective about what is going on with Peter at his soul level. During our first exchange, I was shocked at hearing the tone of his voice as he spoke from his soul, unencumbered by his body, mind, and ego.

Sally: Well, that's very common, Tara. If we spoke to your soul, you might say the same thing. Our souls get so covered up by our bodies, our egos, and our minds that they serve as a veil. And they're obstructing the clear connection, and the communication and the back-and-forth of who we are. So it is often a shock when we get to speak to the pure, unadulterated, spiritual essence, the soul. It's kind of like water in our face — wow, that's really them?

Tara expresses her love for Peter and her willingness to assuage his unfulfilled needs by bringing forth an infusion of love and harmony for a more valuable pattern in their daily routine — one filled with a balance and blend of physical and spiritual choices. She realizes there is an entirely different element of life going on now, and staying busy and doing does not fulfill the opportunity for growth and an energy that opens up doorways to growth and spiritual awareness.

<u>*The following channeled transcription was recorded and transcribed verbatim:*</u>

Tara: Peter was present and given the opportunity to speak in this session, but he declined.

Sally: Tara, you have some specific issues you want to address in this session.

Tara: Yes, I'd like to channel Peter's father, Lewis, who passed about twenty years ago, so that I will have an opportunity to ask him questions that perhaps Peter will want to know the answers.

Sally: Oh sure. I'm sure that that's the truth. I'm sure his father is right handy.

Tara: I did not know Peter's dad for he passed before I met Peter. It is my understanding that Peter's dad experienced a sudden, unexpected, and accidental death. It has troubled Peter for many years. They are very, very close souls.

Sally: I'm sure his dad can talk to us a little about that. We've got to let his dad in now. His dad is here, so let's let him speak. What's his dad's name?

Tara: Lewis.

Sally: Okay, Lewis, come on in here.

Lewis: I'm so excited and feel so astute about the invitation. And I just want you both to know … and precisely I want my Peter to know that ever since I left this planet, I have been with and around him whenever he wants me to and even when he doesn't want me to. That's the amazing difference when we exist without the body than when we have the body. We know we're not constricted by time and space when we're spirit. We just simply flow and fly and be a part of the energy in a deep and joining and wondrous way. So it's amazing, an amazing kind of thing, you know, when you don't feel yourself caught up in the limitations of what the physical is all about.

While I know everyone would have said, "No! Too soon, Lewis; what did you leave for? That was so untimely, so different, so tragic. Here you would, by a mere accident of ingestion take yourself out of this world!" While I will at first admit that, of course, I didn't know in the physical what was happening or what I was doing, I can tell you at this level I was quite sure. And as much as no one wants to hear it, we really do know, as soulful beings, when the jig is up, when our time is winding down and when we're ready to go. Whether we want to believe that in our conscious self or not is not the issue, and I'm not going to sit here and try and convince you. But, I will tell you that there was nothing about my leaving that in some way wasn't most definitely in perfect harmony and exactly as I preferred it.

For I can tell you, I was determined in this life, as Lewis, to not leave in some horrible, step-by-step, take-yourself-out kind of way. I just didn't have it in me. You, Peter, have a different way. You and I both, as the bookends that we are, chose different ways, not only to live our life but different ways to exit it. So I can tell you that while I loved mine, embraced it and have not one iota of regret over it, I know that you're doing the same. You're taking it step by step, taking different processes of letting go of your involvement in the physical world and seeing how it feels each step of the way. I commend you for that, just as I hope you can commend me for doing it the way I did without there having to be any warning or any sense that this was happening. That's why we have so many lifetimes, so we can choose so many different ways to live them and leave them. And that's the truth of it all.

So, I want you to know — both of you; you included in this too, Tara — I'm as every bit present around you as if I was there physically, sitting in a chair, smoking a pipe, looking at you with that keen eye of mine and wanting to engage in conversation. It's really true. We have such a sense of reality and a sense and a way of connecting with each other that most often in the physical world, you're just not open to. You just don't see it; you don't get it.

But for me, the reality is beautiful; it is like I feel everything about you, my son. I feel our strong connection over the eons. I know you, and we have been together countless times, and so we can just immediately feel that give and take. So what I want to say to you is, "Be more aware when you're on the astral plane asleep, Peter. Be aware that I am there, and I'm communicating with you as strongly and deeply as I possibly can." I do it with you too, Tara, but perhaps not with as much intensity as I do Peter, because I want you to know I'm alive, I'm well, I'm vibrant, and I'm perfectly content in how I am. And I just want to be there for both of you to let you know you can get support and strength from those of us who are in the other worlds. I want you to be able to hear this from me, loud and clear, so you'll know there is a reality different than your own. And if you'll only trust it, you'll get the benefit and gifts of it.

Sally: Wo-o-o, he's very good!

Tara: Wow, I loved that; it was great!

Sally: Yeah, you want to ask him something else? Think, what would Peter want to ask? Isn't it interesting? He said, like bookends, trying different ways to leave the planet.

Tara: Yes. Let's ask Lewis about Peter's efforts to again participate in playing a role in state government work so that he could make a difference here in Louisville.

Sally: But what kind of political position was ...

Tara: In 1970, during Peter's late twenties, he became the youngest member of the Kentucky House of Representatives and served a two-year term. Later he became Secretary of the Department of Human Resources in the governor's cabinet. From what Peter told me (I did not know him then when he was in his early thirties), he was so enthralled with being in a place where he could create changes and make a difference. When Peter and I gave up the Florida-based consulting firm and moved back to Louisville in 2003, he wanted to not only retire in Louisville but perform public service work, again; this time in local politics. While Peter was seeking possibilities of serving again, there seemed to be so many blocks; everywhere he turned, the door closed.

Sally: Yeah, his dad is definitely speaking about that.

Lewis [to Peter]: Of course, I have to give my two cents to that, and it was a whole lot better that you didn't go into it, Peter, my son. You gotta hear me. One of the reasons that it's a great gift of leaving ... one of the ones but not just all of the reasons, just one of the ones is that you were on a course that was so mismatched to you. Yes, you thought because you were good ... that's part of the quality of who you were with your brightness and your articulateness and all this stuff that made you drawn to politics. It wasn't that you didn't have the right stuff, but in terms of who you are, that inner voice, that consciousness that you and Sally and Tara have been talking about in terms of soulful essence, *oh, ple-e-ase.* You would not have lasted there. You might have gotten excited by it but eventually you were gonna be so devastated and depleted by that ridiculous system, that law and order, that rule and inflexibility and strictness of energy that comes with politics. And, then having to do what other people want you to do whether you want it or not or whether you think it's right, it would have gotten so out of hand. Who you were, as a soul, you would not have been able to match at all with that kind of life.

So just see, my transition is doing you a favor, my dear son. You didn't have to stay in that energy that would so have been not a match and not a harmony for you. You could have done it and been taken down. And I will tell you, Tara, you would not have been able to put up with him. His energy would have gone to such an arrogant and inflated place that you would have said, "If you don't get out of this, I'm not gonna be here." So see, it went another way, but it went there for a higher reason.

Tara: Oh my gosh. So you see there's always a reason for everything.

Sally: Yes, I get what his dad's saying. He's just saying that it may have looked exciting, and for that stage of his life where Peter was, it was feeling fulfilling and promising, but had he gotten a little older ... and, of course, his dad's kickback ... Whenever anybody dies who is close to us, the kickback to us is to get knocked into more authentic ways of being and behaving. It's so strong that that's what was happening. That kickback to Peter was, "I can't, I don't have the heart to do this," which in the end was good because it would not have been the path for him.

Tara: I'm so glad that Lewis commented on this.

Sally: Well, he certainly did.

Tara: Thank you, Lewis; that's great.

Sally: That *is* great. Good for him. Yeah, you got to hear this, Peter. Your dad is always around you. He's such a guide. He's like a guardian angel kind of a soul, looking out for bringing you whatever he can, you know? You too, Tara, since you do so much of the communicating, or all of it. In your meditation, when you come out of it, I would say, "Okay, Lewis, got any messages for Peter and me?" And then just sorta sit there and write, just see what comes out … because he's very strong and able to do it, and so are you. It's just a matter of getting into practice.

[End of session/tape.]

Chapter 10

Third Exchange
Transcript of December 1, 2011
Channeled by Sally Baldwin, Channel/Medium

Tara passionately expresses her continued efforts to create opportunities for a sense of peace and calm. By providing a balance between time spent alone in meditation and time spent with each other, she is able and willing to achieve this state of harmony. At times, she notes, Peter seems despondent and unhappy with her.

Tara also expresses her wish to speak to Peter's mother.

<u>*The following channeled transcription was recorded and transcribed verbatim:*</u>

Sally: So we'll let Peter's soul in first and then … did you know his mother?

Tara: Yes, I knew her well. She was a wonderful person. She was tough on Peter though. He didn't feel a lot of love and support there.

Sally: Okay, and then you can ask Peter's higher self any question you want, you know. You can have your questioning of him; it doesn't have to be just him volunteering. So, if there's a particular area or something you would like him to expand on, he will. Let's let him in. Come on in, Peter.

Peter: I am full of myself in so many different ways. I am sure that if I were to give you some of the real true inklings of what is going on in here, I would surprise and startle myself as much as I would you. For you don't realize when you're in the body how disconnected you can be from this voice of yourself. I'm so grateful that you're giving me this platform here, Tara; that you're letting me say and express what it is that I feel because there is so much that happens that disconnects. I can't feel the bridge and the link to who I am at this deeper level — what my immortal knowledge is all about to be able to bring it up into the conscious self that lives here as the human called Peter.

So, I recognize and know the real gift and value of this; to be able to shift into the energy that is so deep and loving and so wondrous in terms of who I am at this level, and then have to filter it through all the issues that our egos, minds, and bodies are so consumed by. That can become almost schizophrenic, you know. No wonder you get a sense of my emotions not being terribly uplifting or light. It's because I feel myself in one moment just like I am now, soaring as the spirit I am, and then dragged down into the mud — into the dirt, quickly, by the physical nature of what we're all about here.

So I suppose you might say my real challenge and my real journey at this juncture of my life, is to be able to meld these two, and to better have them balance the idea that I don't have to keep looking at what am I *not* able to do, what am I not living as, as a physical being; and instead, begin to embrace and celebrate what I am as a spiritual being ... not trying to turn into a Pollyanna and make the lemons that I feel in the material world turn into lemonade. No, I don't need that. But, what I do want is to be able to feel the link to this voice — the voice that's speaking to you so openly and honestly now, so I can realize that I am both, both aspects of me, the one that's getting along with or trying to get along with what the physical issues are all about, and this one that doesn't care, that can soar beyond that and just *be*.

This is why it's so important that you join with me on this, that you realize I cannot find the soaring and the depth of energy that is this voice speaking to you when I keep being hauled back into the way the physical is lived here. And, you are the major instrument of that. I'm not saying it with blame or judgment. Believe me, at this level, I have no blame and judgment. What I am saying is that your constant wanting to *help* me is more of something that's doing something for you than it is for me. In truth, you help me more by leaving me to figure out how can I stay in this place that isn't so grounded, isn't so stuck in what the material is all about, and, what it dictates we have to do here.

And when you are not here, I am in more of an inclination to let go, even if it's despondency or depression that takes me there. I don't care what the instrument is that gets me there, my dear. If it has to be a lower emotion, so be it, but I would rather me soar and just feel that energy of choice. Do I get into the physical and material stuff, or do I let it go? But when you are here, you feel such an inclination, such a need to assist me, to help me, that you turn your energy into doing all of that physically. If you could stay with me, and be in my presence and not *do* anything, not make yourself some sort of a sister or helper to me in any way, but just recognize [that] all I want is to sit and be in some part of a day with you — where there's no game, no action, no reaction, nothing to do; that helps me more than anything. And to be able to put that out there with such clarity and such openness is a true gift for me. And, once again, I thank you for that.

Sally [to Tara]: Let me stop for a while. Are you getting this? He's in a particular juncture of his journey from what he's saying, that is basically saying: "All right, I'm trying to get a handle on this and I want to experience more of the ungrounded and the territory I'm not so familiar with as a material being, but you come in and you haul me back into the material." You see? So, if I were to take this into practical implementation, one of the things I would do, Tara, hearing what Peter is saying, is this: I would find some amount of time each day to put on, let's just say as an example a meditation tape, and just sit in the same room with Peter. You don't even have to be where he could see you, but just sitting in the same room, and both of you going through that with your own experience, whatever it is.

What else can Tara do, Peter?

Peter: It's not what *more* can you do; it's what *less* can you do. That's what I'm trying to get across here. I don't need as much care as you might believe I do or that I might even articulate that I wish you'd give me. You know, the physical self, like I said, can get pretty distracted and detached from the spiritual self. And when you're in this state of being *I am*, you have more of an inclination to pick that up and know that to be true. So, what I would say is … it's not so much what more, in addition, can you do with me that isn't so caught up in the doing, it's what can you do less. I know you feel inclined to make sure that I'm cared for, that I am comfortable, and that I have all my needs met; but I know that in some way that becomes more agitating than it does helping me get to a serenity and a place that I can release.

So I suppose I'm saying to you, pay attention and sort of take a look at what is it that you do when the caregivers aren't here. What do you bring to me? What do you attend to with me that you can start slowly letting go of, and not do as much

of — not think that it has to be this certain way because that's what you believe I want. And I'm not saying that it isn't what I want. My physical nature — I do have habits; I do have wants and desires. But, I also know that holding on to them and letting them constantly swirl around me isn't letting me get to that state of release and being-ness that I'm so earnestly seeking, which is why the despondency, why there's such a sense of ... I'm not as happy to see you as you'd like me to be. It's that I know you are the ticket, they're not. They're just doing their job and doing it with a willingness and a sense of connecting with me. I'm fine with that. But you are the one I see as the key to shift it and change it, and the only way you can do that is not do it in that same old way that you think you should. That's the best I can do to give you the advice.

Sally: It doesn't have to be huge and gargantuan, but it's more the intention of the message that you're giving him, you know — that you're willing to not see it in the same old pattern; that you have a different intention with it than you did prior. That is the big change. That is a shift that he can feel in very profound ways, but he can't express it; so you never know it, right?

Tara: Yes, I understand, and I will certainly make a difference by breaking away from the repetition that limits Peter's ability to evolve.

Peter, would it be helpful to turn off the television after dinner and give you some quiet time?

Peter: I would say that you will intuit and know that there are times when I would want the entertainment of what the TV brings me, but there are times too when I can take the quiet. Both could be a balance for me. That's really what I'm looking for here, Tara. Not that I am trying to criticize or judge, but just to let you know that I do want a diversity of experiences and that

it isn't all about me being cared for and being able to stay here on the planet. It's really about my energy and self now. I want to have included a sense of something else is going on beyond what I understand, and I want it to be emphasized every day. And you're the only one I know who can do that.

Tara: Sally, with the intention that I am not just here to make sure Peter's physical needs are met, I am more than willing to be here to bring another kind of energy, a different kind of back and forth. Even though I do not know what it might be just now, I am willing to bring it to my dearest Peter.

Sally: Tara, there are different reasons you and Peter are together now at this stage, and it's not just caregiving. It's like *you* get something out of it … you perhaps choosing a book that you would like to read and then you're reading it out loud to Peter. You're participating in joining with him, but you're also nurturing yourself at the same time, you know? That's the ingredient I feel he's getting at. The piece is … what are *you* getting out of it, and not just the satisfaction of the solace that you're helping him. He gets that. It's also what it is that you're cultivating that is bringing nourishment to *you*.

That's how you want to see it, Tara. Of course, you love him. You want to share the love that you have and show and demonstrate that in your tending to him. That's a given. It's like his soul is saying, his higher self is saying: "I get that, I get it, I get it because you are capable of helping to take us to another level before I leave this planet, before I transition."

You know, it's like stretching you both simultaneously. You take an old habit and pattern that you're in because that's what circumstances in life have dealt you, and take it and transform it by having an intention and a focus that's altered a bit. What I feel his higher self, his soul is saying is to take it to a vibration that includes something else in that picture, and that something else is the intangible, the soulful, and that you don't even have to know what that looks like, Tara. You just have to be willing to declare, "Okay, however that can manifest for you, Peter, I am bringing it. My intention is to know that we're delving into energies of communion on different levels as well as the obvious of what I'm doing for you right now." And when you declare that, and when you mean it, and when you give over to that, that's exactly the altering energy piece that I believe his higher self is talking about.

Tara: Peter, do you enjoy my reading to you?

Sally: Okay, I just said to Peter: "Is the reading astute for you?" And, he went ... yes.

Peter: I would by no means tell you what you have to do, but what I feel would bring us closer in terms of what I'm getting to here is doing the non-typical. Whatever it is that we usually do is a given. And like I have said earlier, I expect that, but it's the unexpected. It's the place where there's spontaneity, serendipity that I want — like you just bringing in ice cream and touching it to my lips, and you drinking down whatever it is you want in the way of a treat. Then *you* begin to give *me* a sense that *I'm* participating in what brings *you* pleasure too. You see, it's so one-sided now, Tara. I feel like you are the one ministering to me, and I bring nothing back to you at all. So, whatever it is that you can set up that you can add into our routine that is not routine at all and is giving you a sense of pleasure; then that alters and changes everything. And I can participate and celebrate that.

Sally: Now that was interesting; do some things that will literally bring *you* joy!

Tara: That's wonderful! When I monitor Peter's emotions, and I see his eyes grow larger and he smiles at me, I believe he is telling me that what I'm doing is pleasing him.

Peter: That's exactly what I mean. I want you to know that it's not that you have to do anything *different*, it's just how you do it and what it is that you feel is the gain of it. It is not just the sensation of having ice cream that gives me any pleasure, or yes, as you see the emotions etched on my face; it's what it is that you bring into the mix. And I don't just want duty and diligence to be a part of it. And I know that you recognize and know that there is a loving energy that can come in many different modes and fashions. And so we're ready for the next mode, the next way of doing this. We can have a sense of you realizing that I have something to give to you and that my circumstances are not just a drain. When I begin to feel that they are, I can't get up out of the resentment and the heaviness of that. That's why the lightness that I get from you, and what it is that you put out there that's more spontaneous and joyful, is when we start making the balance occur; and then it starts feeling better to both of us.

Tara and Sally discuss Peter's daily routine, the issues involved, and ways for Tara to take time out for herself.

Peter: I'm not content with what it is I am about now, not for the obvious reasons of my lack of functioning, but because I know I feel like I am just *existing*. That's nothing you can do anything about, but what you can do is as we are discussing. And as much as I'm trying to make it as clear as I can, I hear that I am not getting through. What I want you to hear is that you don't have to set up everything about this system of obligation to me. And as much as you say you want to show how you care, there is also

so much obligatory energy in this. You can't help it. It would be anybody's fate who is going through this kind of routine and this kind of partnership. So, all I'm saying is just shoot down the routine and begin to do things out of the order that they have been set for so long. And while that, at first, may seem disconcerting to you or you get some sort of reaction from me in the physical, pay it no attention. Just follow whatever it is you can do to begin to change it up, for in the changing it up, we both benefit. You just have to trust me on this. This is what I know.

Tara explains that when she takes time out for herself, anxious feelings surface. If something happens to Peter in her absence, she will not be there with the caregiver to help Peter and make a decision on what to do.

Peter: I can tell you honestly, my dear, that I have more of a close intimacy with what the other side is about than I'm able to tell you. All of my little forays into the dimensions have helped me become accustomed and secure in the fact that I'm going to be cared for. I don't have to be afraid. So you just know that whatever it is that I decide to use as my final exit, it will be something that will be smooth enough between us. You won't have to feel that there was something shocking or difficult that you didn't attend to. I'll make sure it goes smoothly as long as *you* make sure you don't stay fearful and anxious about it.

Sally: He feels it; he feels it too. And so he's just assuring you, letting you know it's okay, so you don't have to do the up-and-down, back-and-forth worry thing. Very good, that was good Peter.

His mother is here. Peter, your mother, is here! Tara, what is her name?

Tara: Irene.

Irene: I am just not as old a being. I don't find myself entering into the physical human world with a lot of wisdom. I'm not saying that as an excuse to either of you, or you especially, my dear son, so that you can sorta forgive me and make excuses for me as [your] mother. I will tell you though that I can be unapologetic at this point for I know that I did the best I could. But I also know that I just didn't carry the wisdom with me that others do. And I didn't have the instinct and the know-how to handle not only motherhood but just handle, with some sort of aplomb, the idea of being in the physical as a human being. It really didn't sit so well with me. So, of course, there were rough patches; of course there were jagged edges.

I'm here to just tell you now that that didn't get in the way of me loving you from the first moment I held you. I really did the best I could with love; I just didn't know how to engender the kind of emotional closeness that we all look for. I didn't really have it given to me, so I wasn't very prepared to be able to give it to you or anybody else. I just want to be able to say that, so you'd know that you can let go in peace, realizing I gave you everything I could. But it wasn't nearly enough of what you were capable of and what you wanted.

So let me just say that to both of you. I want you to recognize and know that I see things now I didn't when I was there, and that I still couldn't have done it any different because that's who I was.

Tara: I'm so happy to hear Irene speak to us. Wasn't that great of her to ...

Sally: Yeah, that took a lot for her to push in and leap into that.

Tara: I loved her, and I think she liked ... loved me.

Irene: I most certainly do. It's not in the past tense, my dear, for we still feel, we feel the flow of love back and forth whether we're in a body or not. I'm saying that to you, my son, too, for I do realize and know that you can't know things the way that we can when we're no longer in the body. But I can tell you I'm present, I'm close, and I'm bringing as much love into the mix for you two as I possibly can.

Tara: Oh, thank you so much, Irene. And Sally, isn't that beautiful?

Sally: It *was* beautiful; good for you, Irene.

Tara: I believe I have learned a lot today where my dear, wonderful Peter is concerned.

Sally: That's very good, Tara. You've got a little bit of a challenge on your plate for you to shift it up some. You've got the capacity, and you're ready to hear this.

Tara: Thank you, Sally. Thank you so much, Peter, for this enlightening and spiritual insight. I love you.

[End of session/tape.]

Chapter 11

Fourth Exchange
Transcript of April 30, 2012
Channeled by Sally Baldwin, Channel/Medium

Tara opens by expressing her love for Peter and her gratitude for this wonderful opportunity to commune. She relates to him her thoughts about shifting the focus to breaking out of the old routine and creating profound changes for the highest and best energy that each one needs. There is now an understanding that Peter is at a particular juncture in his journey in which he wants to experience more of the ungrounded territory that he is not so familiar with as a material being.

The following channeled transcription was recorded and transcribed verbatim:

Sally: Let's see what Peter wants to say. Come on in, Peter.

Peter: I would say that most definitely, what we are feeling together is not so much understanding as [it is a] willingness to experience where the other one is right now, without any regard to our own desire or to have our needs fulfilled. That's really what it feels like to me, is that you could just have experience for experience sake, and that is a beautiful and pure kind of thing. Don't you agree that we don't have to get caught up in what is

it that we want; and are we gonna get there, and are you gonna instruct me, and are you gonna realize what I want? All of that is dissipating now and doesn't really have a place in my life anymore.

So what you're describing is for the pure experience of whatever the experience is, you and I are exchanging energy. *That's* the difference, my dear, not so much about understanding anything although I know that's the word we love as we are in the human condition. But I can tell you that what *really* makes a difference for me is when you can just release to it. This is the experience, nothing more, nothing less. I'm just going to flow with it. There we are in that beautiful place where you can find serenity, you can feel the love, and you can trust and know that something greater than who we both are is happening. That's where I'm going more and more now, and it feels so gratifying to realize that you're working so diligently to be there with me.

Sally: Yeah, and to the degree, Tara, that you can keep moving in that direction to not always be trying to get to something on the other side, to get to the end, but rather, be as you've heard so many times from the Buddha … *be in the moment* of what you're doing or what you're focusing on, no matter how mundane or insignificant the task. Then, that's what he's talking about. You're not trying to understand it; you're not trying to make it be, as he said, accepted by the other person. You're just totally present to the moment. And, of course, that's all you've got, so he's going to value that. Now you're the one that has to kinda calibrate and alter yourself and adjust to that because you still have got so many things going on in your head, and what you see needs to be done and all this stuff we all go through.

He really is accentuating how much that kind of behavior and energy tears us away from the true, authentic reason we're here.

You know, it's to exchange and experience the energy together, not to get to an end point or to finish this task as we like to put it in our humanity, you know. So it's very wise and a great reminder. Whatever is happening with him inside is softening and is flowing more with the energy than it is with the material world, like or dislike, acceptance or not acceptance. So that's really good, and you can feel that in what he's saying.

Peter: Just know, that when you go to the worry place, then you put up the wall that says: *Okay, I can't flow, I can't find the real wonderment in this exchange.* **Then, of course, that's what I hit. I go into that wall because worry or anxiety or any kind of fearful manifestation of those kinds of emotions is going to bring up a wall; it's what it always does. So I sense and feel your fear-worry, and then, of course, we play the game smacking into the walls, you know. And I know that that's not something we want to give the rest of my time to here. We want to have as little of that kind of going-on as possible.**

So, I am one to say to you, when you feel a bit worried, or you feel concerned, go and do whatever you need to do to let go of that and release it. And don't feel that you have to stay in my presence, because whatever the worry or concern is, I'd much prefer you take yourself out and around and away from me so that you can be in tune with what it is that's got you riled and get it more settled down and back to neutral. Then when you come back into my presence, I don't have to feel the worry or the anxiety of the concern. I can just feel that there you are giving your energy to me, having the exchange of that experience.

Sally: Tara, what you're really doing is working on you to realize that the soul knows when the soul's ready to go, and that's regardless of how the death occurs or how old the person is when they die. You know it's as true for a newborn baby as it is for an eighty-year-old man; and that we have to come to some real acceptance of so that we don't do what he's talking about — throw out the worry and the fear and the concern to the point that then we hold back the great wisdom and the great excitement of the soul going to the other side. That's the greatest event; the greatest event that we participate in here on the Earth. Although if you talk to the ego side of our culture especially, it's about being born, the birth. But to the soul, it's going the other way where it's the real excitement and the real joy.

Tara: I love Peter so much.

Sally: And he loves you too. So, it's a grand partnership when you can do this, when you can be, you know, when you can really go to the soulful, spiritual level and say: *It's just as important what we're exchanging there as whatever we're exchanging here in the physical.*

Tara: Peter, thank you for showing me what is needed to take us to a whole different level. I love you deeply. And, thank you, Sally. I'm so grateful for your love, the continual guidance you give us, and your words of wisdom.

[End of session/tape.]

Chapter 12

Just Being In The Moment, Soul-to-Soul

When your loved one's soul is choosing a path to the spiritual realm through illness, this is your time to be *in the moment* with her or him. Try to stop and think about what this means. If your loved one wants to express deeply held feelings about what she or he is going through, take the time to be there with compassion and understanding. Try to see that someone in this condition of failing health can initially be frightened. Your loved one has time to think about what is going on inside and may be asking himself questions. Be supportive when approached with downcast feelings and comments, such as the two that my husband said to me, very early on, that were so poignant that I cannot forget them. Peter said, "I wonder if I'll make it." And, at another time he said, "I don't want to miss out on anything." I remember how my heart sank when I heard these words. Struck by the message these words carried, his self-doubt appeared much worse than I had previously envisioned. It seemed to be showing his vigilance in observing the seriousness of his condition. I recall reminding myself of the importance of providing nourishing love and support when he was feeling afraid. Whatever else was going on at that moment could surely wait.

When you remember this is your time to be with your loved one, you can *always* get back to whatever you were *doing*. Realize that these are the moments you will cherish, knowing you were there for comfort, support and validation at the time needed. When your loved one wonders or asks about the changes his body is experiencing, offer him your full attention. Even though you may not understand the situation or know the answer, you can be there in an exchange of the energy of soulful love and support. Just being present in the moment is transcending all thoughts and personal history and integrating your individual sense of self with your heart, intuition, and love — while connecting spiritually.

As another way of repeating what I have previously said, awaken the soulful connection between you and your loved one. Allow love and harmony to flow and replace any negative emotions — only see the beautiful and compassionate being that we are and see through their outer facade of personality. *Just Being in the moment* is feeling the exchange of energy on a soul-to-soul level and realizing that this is your time to be with your loved one. While the usual, necessary daily routine of physical caregiving duties is important, it need not take precedence over the attention given to the questions and concerns of your loved one's inner soul. Be sensitive to his fears about losing hope, be conscientious to his concerns about how his life is changing, and be compassionate with his fears about losing his life. Tuning-in to those moments and embracing the capacities of your internal abilities within divine consciousness can stir your heart's emotions. It will allow you to embrace your loved one's best interests and extend an infusion of much-needed love and support … *for both of you.*

Chapter 13

Fifth Exchange

(Approximately Eight Months before Peter's Transition)
Transcript of March 16, 2013
Channeled by Laura Mirante, Channel/Medium

Tara: Our beloved channel/medium, Sally Baldwin passed on June 6, 2012. Peter and I declare our continued love and gratitude for Sally's immeasurable support of our spiritual journey. (All further references to Sally or her channeled voice are signified as, Sally*.)

Tara declares her love for Peter and appreciation for his many gifts of beautiful energy and love. She apologizes for the interruption in the continuum of channeled communications due to time spent creating a space for our new channel/medium, Laura Mirante.

Tara thanks Laura for this exciting opportunity to again venture into an interdimensional realm with Peter. She acquaints Laura with Peter's compromised condition, his inability to use his human voice, and the background information regarding their previous four channels with Sally.*

Laura Mirante explains there is no separation between channeling with Sally and channeling with her. She assures Tara that although*

Peter's human voice was taken away, he speaks from his soul awareness.

Tara offers Peter the platform.

<u>*The following channeled transcription was*</u>
<u>*recorded and transcribed verbatim:*</u>

Peter: Dear one, I do see how you have offered me this space so that I can communicate with you. And I do recognize that my previous communications have allowed you to see how I am moving through this experience with a sense of growth and opportunity here. I do see it more as an opportunity for my soul to experience life in a way that I may never have allowed myself if I had not had these illnesses come upon me. So I do give you my gratitude for continually supporting me on this journey and allowing me to have the freedom that you are able to give me. And I want you to know that I do recognize how much you give of yourself and how often you stay focused on my wishes although they may not concur with what your heart is asking of you. And I say, thank you.

And, I do hope that I have not caused you too much difficulty, for I can only imagine what it is I am to you in this moment, and how I affect your ability to define for yourself a new energy to create in. But what I am realizing is that *we* are creating this new energy together and that I am not in this experience alone but rather that *we* are in this experience together. This is something I have come to see now. This is what I have been ruminating over for some time. This is not just *my* experience at all, but rather this is *our* experience. And, I want you to realize that I have recognized this, and I am giving you a moment here to realize

this yourself, that it is not just about me, that this and everything I am going through is affecting *you* as it affects me, maybe not in the same physical way as I, but it does have an emotional impact on you.

It does have a physical impact on you, and it is affecting your ability to communicate in the world with others like we used to. You have detached from many of those that you associated with, and you have distanced yourself from many people that feel they can offer you a moment of relief just by having an exchange. And, so I would ask you to have those moments with others, to have those conversations, to have those interactions where you do not feel that all of your thoughts have to be on me; where you can go to a different place in your mind, and you can have other distractions, so that you can be in an energy other than mine and my situation.

I know, for a while, I gave you the idea that it was for me that I wanted the space, and yes, that is true. I am able to go to a higher awareness when I sit with myself for some time. And what I understand is that is something that everybody can do if they take the time to sit with themselves, but that is not what I am asking of you. Rather, I ask that you sit with others, that you have more communications with others, more relations, and more interactions so that you are not so disconnected from everyone when I do take my leave. That is a consideration I am holding now, and it is a concern of mine, so I want to let you know this.

I am also experiencing a different *kind* of energy now. I am *aware* of what is occurring around me, but now it is much more distant than it used to be. It isn't as though I feel so connected to it like I used to be. I feel as though I am much more the observer now than the participant in this life. And so if you feel as though there's a depth in my eyes that didn't previously exist, it is because I am expanding more fully into the awareness of the higher self. And, I *am* recognizing that I am more than my physicality, and that I can be here as an observer watching and experiencing life through the other senses; the other senses that have not been identified through science.

Dear one, I can see how I appear to others. That is what I want to say to you. I am at that place now where I can actually see how others perceive me. And I do not mean see with my eyes in the physical, but rather I know it on a different level because I have opened up to that other, or those other levels of who I am. I am able to perceive me through the awareness of those around me or who are engaged in my experience.

And I am amazed at how limited the human — oh, wow, the human understanding of what it is I am going through truly is. People do not realize that this is a magnificent experience for the soul. And although I do relish in my memories of my strongest times, in my physicality, and I do remember when I was able to do just about anything I set my mind to, and I do long for another time in another life in another incarnation where I may feel that vitality once again; in this moment, I cannot say that I am feeling less than, or that I feel that I am missing anything. Yes, I may seem that way to others in the physical, but I am experiencing life through new eyes. I am experiencing life through *new* senses, and it is such an exciting journey; a journey of self-discovery, one that allows me to know myself on a much deeper level than most humans do because they get stuck in those five senses. They don't even seek out the other senses that we all do have, and we all are aware of at times in our lives.

Peter [to Laura]: Delivering this information is very exciting, interesting, and deliberate, for I feel as though this channel is a part of the other channel [with Sally*]. And it doesn't feel like there is any shift here. There is an intensity here that I did not feel with Sally* that I see is an intention to be as open as one can be. And this is almost intimidating, for the intention to do it accurately is overwhelming me. And so I would say to you, dear Laura, it is not as difficult as you thought, and it is working out just fine.

Laura [to Peter]: I know, I know, I was worried. Yeah, thank you, Peter.

Peter: Well, certainly there is room for this kind of exchange here, isn't there? When we all gather in this way there really is more to be said than what we can put into words, isn't there? It is something that we are all experiencing here, and now that I experienced Sally* in this way, I want to bring that to you too, Tara. There is a sense here that Sally* is always with me. It is quite interesting to know her on this level now that I have met her in her human form as Sally*. But what I see here is an expansiveness that goes so far beyond the human being you and I met in those exchanges. She is a wondrous expression of light and love and one that is engaged in the physical world with such an impenetrable devotion to connecting souls regardless of what form they are in. It does not matter if I am here or there, she is willing to be a bridge for me regardless of my situation, and this is what I see from her for so many people. And I want to tell you that. I want to tell you both that, for it is amazing to know her on this level, and that is what I am capable of doing now.

I am capable of maneuvering the earth plane through the energetic links that we have to other people. *That* is what I

am experiencing now, as well, that I wanted to share; that I can, through you, feel the intentional energies of those around us. I feel the family through your connection to them, and I feel their energies moving through our connection. It is quite interesting, and I know I may not be explaining it exactly as I am experiencing it, but I wanted to give you a sense of it. When another comes to visit, I see them through your energy field because you and I have that kind of connection that communicates without hesitation. And, others, well others are so hesitant in approaching and so hesitant in expressing their truth to me that it is, ah, [laughter] it is quite humorous to see what it is that comes out of their mouths when I can know what it is they have in their hearts.

Tara comments about how beautiful and remarkable it is to know Peter feels the intentional energies of others through her; and that he is communicating with Sally's* soul on a different level now.

Peter: I *can* expand, my dear. I can expand even further to give you a sense of how *ethereal* we really all are, and how embedded in this illusion our mind becomes, which is exactly why we can't find our way to this truth because we get so stuck in our minds. And isn't it interesting? … someone like me who loved to come from logic would be having this conversation with you now at this point on our journey. It is really, really an exploration of self that I have taken. I have *allowed* myself to distance myself from the logic, so that I *can* maneuver through the maze of confusion it creates within our being-ness; so that I can then find my way to the higher self which illuminates for me my connection to others.

That seems to be the way it's worked. It was like a journey through the mind, and it lead me to my highest self which leads me to *all others* in life, all others in human form and in spiritual form. That is the beauty of it, and I am here in the physical still, but I am realizing my connection to those that we know in spirit. And it is as if I did not have to leave the body to do it. I did not *have* to journey all the way home to meet my loved ones again in spirit. I can be here and there at the same time. That is what I am realizing.

And, I will take it one step further and say that this *is* what is available to all human beings if they take that time to step away from logic [and] bring their energy back inward, rather than externally focused; so that they can then find the connection to their higher self which will indelibly bring them to their connection to all life.

So, as *I* journey in my mind, or *through* my mind, I like that — as I journey *through* my mind, I engage you. Of course, my dear, and I bring you with me. I have developed a plan where I know exactly how to do it. I have figured out how to maneuver through this maze of confusion, and into the light so that I can find my way to the higher awareness that then illuminates for me, exactly why it is I am experiencing this and what I can benefit from it, in that exact moment. And I believe that that is how life is meant to be lived regardless of our situation, without the need for illness. I believe now that all human beings can do this, can take themselves out of the details of the experience and pull themselves away far enough so they can become the observer of the experience. And then they can grow as the souls that they are, through the human experience. That is what is occurring with me. I am taking this awareness with me. I would not do all of this to just come back and have a similarly limited fear-based experience. I will take this, and I will assimilate it into my soul so that I know when I come back, I will reflect this kind of awareness in whatever human form I take.

Ah, there is that opportunity to take what we have learned here and integrate it in a manner that allows us to benefit from it in future experiences. And that is how we grow as the souls that we are, that is how we expand our awareness of what is possible as energy in physical form. It really is quite fascinating. And, it is an amazing experience to have, especially with this kind of freedom to speak from the soul level where I do not have to put it in the human terms about *how I feel* and *where it hurts,* but rather, where I look to expand, and how I look to engage others in this life. Can you feel the difference in that? Can you see how it has shifted my interpretation of what this life is all about?

Now if only we could share this kind of information with others and allow people to benefit from my experience. Well, that certainly would be something, wouldn't it, to know that I went through this so that others can realize that there is no loss of self when something like this happens, that the self itself is actually *expanding* because of the experience. You see, so many people in the physical think otherwise, don't they? They look at me and they think, *wow, what is left of this man? There is little left of the man we once knew.* And yet, are they looking at the soul? Are they seeing me as the total being that I am, or, are they evaluating my situation by what I am expressing in the physical?

Ah, there is so much more to every human being than we know, my dear. And I would say to you, look for that in each person regardless of what it is they are putting forth. Look beyond the surface expression and into the depths of their being-ness that exists in their eyes, for that is where the truth lives. And, anyone that looks into my eyes knows now that I am here in my soul experiencing life from this point of view; the detached state of knowing that says, *I do not have to engage this physical world, in the same way that you do to have the experience I came to have.*

Laura: It feels like Peter has expanded, and there was a shift. Peter has surrendered to it by working through the mind before he could get to the higher self, and then to the higher awareness that then connected him into the connection to all life. Peter, that was brilliant, just brilliant.

Peter: I have applied my persistence, my dedication, [and] my devotion to this endeavor. I have realized that this is what it is about for me. It is not about me trying to find the way to heal myself or to heal my physicality. I have given over all of my energy to understanding what it is I am experiencing, why it is I am experiencing it, how it is affecting me and those around me, and how it is affecting all life. That's where I am taking it. And I am using every bit of my tenacity to do this kind of venturing forward so that I can understand it, so that I can embrace it, and, so that I can share it with you.

Remember this. I am trying to give you that sense that this is not just for me or about me, but that we, my dear, decided to do this together; that we came into this life with full awareness that at some point, we would be having an experience such as this. And, yes, we may not have known that as small children, or even as adults when we came together. But *we did* know this as the souls that we were, that we were going to take ourselves out of the limitations of this physical experience and see how far we could expand into our truth. And *that* is what we are doing now.

As I expand into it through my experience, I bring it right back to you so that you can then use the information and energy that I bring back with the information to expand within your

own self. Everything I say here that I am experiencing, *you* are capable of experiencing too but without the illness. That is what I want to say to you so that when I do take my leave, I know we will have that connection. We will have that connection similar to what Laura was saying she and Sally* have where there is no separation. There is no sense that I am *gone* but rather I have just *shifted forms*. That's the kind of relationship I want to have in our future, and so we are laying the groundwork now.

Tara: It's amazing! I've dreamed it would be that way. Thank you, Peter.

Laura: So while you were dreaming it, he was figuring it out!

Peter: As you *are* beginning to realize, this dream state is a way for you to elevate your frequency to shift away from logic and to begin to learn how to connect on a spiritual level. That's what happens when we go to sleep. We shut the mind, and we elevate our frequency, so we *can* commune there on the astral plane. Do not take it so literally, at first. But I would say we have much to look forward to now in our investigative process as to how we can communicate. Because, my dear, if we can begin this now, if we can begin this while I'm still here, we can just shift more fully into it when I transition. So let's take the time and let's see how we can begin to intuit each other, and let's see if we can connect on the astral plane through your dream state. Again I will say, do not take what you *see* as literal but rather how you interpret it. As you speak your dreams or write your dreams, listen to it or read it back, and see what it might mean to you from an observer's point of view. And follow the *feeling* of it, that's the other thing. We are more deeply connected within our being-ness which serves us through our feelings. So remember that it will be in the *feeling* and how you feel about what is said rather than

the actual literal interpretation of what is being said or conveyed in the dream state.

There is a process that we can go through while I am in this state, that will have us beginning to connect or commune on the higher level of awareness, where you sit with me in stillness, and you focus in your mind on nothing, on nothing but being open to receive. The more we do this, my dear, the more my energy can begin to commune with you in that way and give you a sense of what is occurring within me.

Tara: Yes. Peter ... I am trying to reach you in this way and ...

Peter: I would say try less, my dear, try less, for when you are *trying,* you are *focused* on trying. Can you see how that works? And we must create an openness, a spaciousness, a mind filled with acceptance of whatever is. You see when you *try,* there is an expectation attached to the focus of trying and that is what I want you to let go of. Do not expect to hear my voice in your head, do not expect to see images, and do not expect to get a message, but rather expect to commune in the energy. Because then that leaves you open for you have no idea what that means, do you? And so then you can say, "Okay, I am here, open and curious to see what it means to commune energetically." Then you leave the space that opens to allow me to come through in whatever way I can manage.

At this moment, my dear, this is an investigatory process. We are in the beginning stages. I do not expect anything from you, and I do not want you to put any kind of pressure on you. I, in no way, wanted to give you any kind of stress or homework here. There is no goal that we are looking to achieve. What it is you will be doing is just creating an openness, that is all that is there. There is no effort that needs to be made other than to step away from your thoughts and your focused intentions. You just want to be an open vessel to receive, and it does not matter if that day or any other day you feel like you receive something.

The effort is going to show more in the energy than when it will in the physical, so please do not burden yourself with any kind of expectation of what you think should be. That is something for the higher self to be concerned with and not you, not you the human being. You just want to make this space for the higher selves to begin to dance in the energy. Think of it that way, my dear — it's a new way for us to *dance,* and you do not have to think about where you put your feet. You just have to think of how I can fall into your arms and we can then dance together.

Tara: Thank you, my love; it can't get any more beautiful.

Peter: I can say that there is a desire that exists within both of us to be a part of this experience together. And I do not for one minute want you to think that if I leave my body, I have left you and that I will not be a part of this experience. That's something I want you to know for sure, which is why I am making this effort here, today, to give you this kind of information, so that in my moment of transition you feel me, and you feel me standing there with you, not leaving you somewhere all alone. That's the only purpose I have here is to continue to let you know how connected we truly are because of my ability now to see it so clearly within my own experience.

I am capable of being here and there simultaneously, or at least that's what it appears to me. I do not see the movements of time so definitively any more. I am no longer restricted by it, so it doesn't bother me if I step in or out of my body for five minutes or five hours. I just go, and when I return, I return, and it doesn't seem that too much has shifted in there in the physical when I am gone. So I never really know how long I've been gone, or how far I go — I just know that I am going more fully. I am going more completely.

And I am realizing more now than I did in the past, that we are not, and never were, ever alone or disconnected from the source of life, from our creator. We have always been a part of that creative source, and we have always been supported by it. And although it may not have always appeared so in the physical, it truly is a divine plan that we are working through, and there truly is a purpose behind all experiences.

This is what I am learning as I commune with the others here in spirit, such as Sally*. She has educated me in ways that would have taken years if I were there in the physical, for she would have had to have broken through those logical barriers that I held on to so tightly. It would not be so easy for me to intellectualize all of this that I am bringing to you now, which is why I am doing this, and you are doing that. For the other way around, I just don't know if I would have had it *in* me to bring *you* to this kind of exchange. So I honor you, my dear. I honor you for finding this kind of method of communication — for allowing me to express myself in this way. And I honor you for being able to go with it and not deny it because of fear or fearful logic that we have both grown up so ingrained with.

There is a sense here, that as we continue this journey, and as we continue to develop our ability to interact on different levels of self, we will begin to have that kind of knowingness between us, where I do not have to speak, and you *are* able to know what it is I am referencing through my energy. I do it now, and you get a sense of it. You often times react to what it is I am energetically conveying. Not that you would know it, not that you would give yourself credit for it either, [but] I'm going to say that you really can give yourself much more credit than you do, for knowing what it is I am conveying to you. You are often doubting and often questioning whether you heard me right. I am here to say that more often than not, you do. And even when you don't even know it, you are doing it. And that is why I love you because you are so open to receive my communications even when you don't think you are. There is a part of you that is just assimilating and processing without any acknowledgment. That is how you move about my life, my dear, as this sweet bridge to life that you are.

Tara: My heart feels your love in the way that you said that. Thank you, Peter. I believe I can do even more now.

Peter: That is exactly why I am bringing this information to you, for once we create the belief in your *mind* — *that* energy *alone* creates an opening — it will happen. It really does have some power, the idea of faith. Ah, … the energy of faith is really quite something when you are working in the fields of light that cannot be seen. There is nothing stronger than the faith, my dear. So, have the faith in you that I have in you, and you will see what it is we can do, and you will feel what it is I know. That is the way I will convey things to you, not that you will be able to intellectualize much of what it is I am conveying to you. And you will find that it's not necessary all of the time, although, in your excitement, you will want to share it with others. And many will not be able to understand or process it, but it is really for you and I and that is why we are having the experience. So do not feel that you have to share it if you do not want to.

But do allow yourself an outlet. Do give yourself the opportunity to express yourself to others. It is important for you. I'm going to reiterate the idea that you need human contact with

others. It is quite important, and I want you to consider what I am saying and why I am saying it. And please allow yourself to have that kind of interaction with another. The energy created when you interact with another allows you to become distracted for a moment. It takes your focus off of me and our situation and your efforts at trying to reach me, and then what that does is clean the slate. Can you see that? Begin with a wide-open free awareness, one that is not so bogged down with the intellectualizing of your efforts, so there is a benefit to me in your interacting with others. It's not that you're taking away from your effort with me, but, rather, it will benefit your efforts to know that you can energize yourself through communications with others. And then you can be refueled to come back and give it another go.

Laura: Tara, is there anything you want to ask Peter?

Tara: Peter, do I give you enough time alone to expand your awareness in the spiritual world?

Peter: I feel like there is *ample* time for me to journey in my mind now. And I do not want it to be so stressful for you to feel as though you have to create it for me. I want you to be more at ease with it. I do not want you to feel that I do not want you with me, or, that you are a distraction to me, but rather that there are moments that I can go a little bit further if I am just with myself. Like I said to you, for all human beings, it's just that once in a while, we need to reconnect within our own being-ness, with our higher self, and, that's just one way to do it. So yes, I would say you give me ample time and do not worry about following a structured, rigid schedule. I do not need it to be just so.

Tara: Laura, recently Peter was diagnosed with gastroesophageal reflux disease. We decided to try using the drug, Prilosec, but I don't know if it has helped. Peter, are you in any pain now?

Peter: There is a sense that this is an immediate issue that is being addressed but there are alternatives that I see would do a much better job at allowing me to heal than what this does. It seems to mask the issue rather than deal with it; that's what I will say to you. I cannot give you details on how to go about it, but I know, energetically, there are more healing remedies that would help to heal the issue rather than mask the problem. And so just because they do not see the symptoms does not mean that the issue has gone away. I'll just tell you that, and I won't say that it's too uncomfortable for me. I can say that it is disrupting my ability to digest properly. There's something to that, and it may begin to cause some intestinal issues if not dealt with properly. So I would ask that you do research a little bit on how to heal more holistically, this area of the body and the digestive tract as a whole, for it is not an isolated area that I have this issue.

Tara: I will research the avenues to a more easily tolerated and organic food diet for you, Peter.

Peter: It's an acidity issue. It's an acidity that is created by the environment in which I digest my food, and it is about the lack of alkaline substances in the environment that is creating this acidity that is creating the symptoms. And so again, I bring you back to the issue at hand, which is not to calm the waters but rather to change the structure of the waters.

Laura: Tara, we should look for foods with a balance between alkaline and acid.

Tara: Yes, I too think that's what Peter is telling us. For many years, Peter's diet was not so good until I began introducing a healthier way of eating.

Peter: What I will tell you is this is not an overnight kind of situation. This did not develop just recently. It has been brewing

in my body for some time, my dear, so do not feel it is what you are feeding me. But, rather as you have said, it has been a progressive response to the way I have treated my body over the years.

I am continually grateful, each and every day, for all that you do for me, for all that you give to me, and for all that you share with me. And I want you to know that this is how it is for us, that is how we have defined this life. It is our life; it is ours to share, and it always will be regardless of the form our energy is taking. Our energy is joined, and it will never be separated.

Tara: Oh, that is so beautiful and so profound. I am feeling overwhelmed and grateful for all that you share with me, all the ways that you inspire me. Thank you, Peter. I love you, and I honor you.

[End of session/tape.]

Chapter 14

Sixth Exchange

(Approximately Six Months before Peter's Transition)
Transcript of May 15, 2013
Channeled by Laura Mirante, Channel/Medium

Tara expresses her love and deep concerns that Peter is very ill now and fighting an infection. She wants to know where Peter's soul is, and what measures (if any) he wishes her to take to accommodate his condition.

Tara offers the platform to Peter.

The following channeled transcription was recorded and transcribed verbatim:

Peter: Getting into a new state of mind becomes quite interesting, and [it is] definitely a challenge to my physicality. So, I am grateful to you for this opportunity to give you a sense of what it is I am experiencing and how it is I will move through this next transitional phase of my journey. A certain amount of emphasis must be placed here on this idea of this being a phase of my journey, for I am no longer in the same energy I was before the infections began. I am in a different elevated frequency now; one that is bringing into my awareness a sense of my intentions as a

soul, to begin to move more fully into the transitional energy of my release from this current state of mind.

And so, I say to you dear Tara, find in your deepest connection to me a sense of my willingness to continue to engage this physical experience for as long as I feel that I am still exploring the depth of my being-ness. For with each new adventure, with each new turn in my physical well-being, I bring forth a new level of self-discovery — as I explore my own willingness as a human being that I am, to continue to move through these physical experiences as a part of the extrapolation of my individuality. And, yes, that is what I am experiencing in the deeper parts of my mental acuity; an integrative understanding of how my body affects my mind, my mind affects my energy, and my energy affects both my body and my mind.

I am here in this moment, experiencing just this, this idea that day in and day out, I am continually experiencing new adventures, new challenges, new paths of self-exploration. And I can only tell you that in my deepest sense of knowing, I have found that my more egotistical aspect is certainly rebelling against the idea that I am here to continue this journey, in this manner with no ability to affect my condition in a logical, practical, or even physical manner. I am, as the egotistical man that I am, still fighting with this idea that I must let go of control of everything and give my physicality over to you, my dear. I must surrender my will to what is now your will and what is becoming our will, for I no longer can see my individual egotistically driven will as what drives my intentions.

And, so, what I have put forth as far as the intention to let go of my physicality, as soon as I am presented with this opportunity, I would say that I still hold this frequency in me. I still look to let go and be free once I feel it is truly determined by the higher powers that I am fulfilled in my physical experience. For you see, as the human being, there is an aspect of me that would ask that you initiate the process, that you instigate it even. But, as I know that this is not something that is accepted in our world, I do not request any such measures. I hold still true to the idea that I do not want any extremes taken. I do not want any apparatus affixed to my physicality in order to keep my physicality moving; for I do not feel it would be the same experience. And I do not feel it would bring either of us any sense of comfort or connection.

I can say that in this moment, I am more aware of what I am experiencing than I had been previously. And, although I am unable to encapsulate my awareness in words or give you a sense of my conscious recognition of what is occurring, I do feel that in moments, you recognize my awe; my awe in the moments that I have a clear recognition of myself as the physical being that I am. I feel that you have glimpsed it in moments. And you have allowed yourself to hold on to that part of me that has always been a part of us, so that we can move into this transitional period of life together and can feel this state of knowing regardless of our inability to communicate.

As you know, it is up to you to make the effort to clear the mind so that we may communicate energetically. It is up to you to allow yourself to believe you are entitled to take that time to pull away from me and my experience, if even only for a moment, so that you may sit in the stillness of your own being-ness and become more aware of the energy that you are, which is the energy that connects us.

Everything is directed by the higher self and overlooked by the creator of this experience. We are always in conjunction with the higher aspects of self that are moving us along this journey and into the more expansive experiences so that we can bridge the gaps we created in other lifetimes; so that we can come together as one, knowing we are one and not seeing two individuals coming close, but rather one individual coming back into its own state of expression.

I am establishing for you a sense of my clarity now so that you may know that I am aware in the higher levels of self. I am completely aware of what it is I am experiencing, how I am affecting you and those around us, and what it is I am holding as my intention for the future. And so, as I can, I will share with you what I feel I am able to bring into this experience and allow you to recognize as our truth unfolding before us.

Let yourself be guided by the knowledge that arises from the heart, for that is where I speak to you. That is where I communicate my will, my desire and my intention. That is where I can meet you now. And it is a true adventure for us as souls to bridge this gap that exists between us as the individual union of light that we are, through this intention to connect on another level, a level beyond logic.

And, although it is much more difficult for you to achieve this lightness because of the situation you are in, and because of the need for you to rely on logic, at this moment in our journey, it is difficult for you to find the calmness of mind that will open the doors between us. And, so, I reiterate that this is a time for you to take a few minutes each day to be still, to be silent in [your] mind, and to be open to an energetic communing that will allow us to create a presence among us that will exist beyond my physical life.

My dear, I have seen this extension of your energy. I have recognized how you are aware of the effort you are making. And

I am aware that my energy influences yours, that my ability to connect beyond logic is strengthening, and I am becoming more adept at moving through these different dimensions that exist within us. And, I am aware that as I sit in your presence, I affect your ability to feel the oneness, the stillness, the silence because in my field are so many questions, so many answers, and so many experiences that are churning up the energetic imprints I have experienced in this lifetime. It is as if I am in a process now of reviewing the life I lived, even though I am still living it. It really is an amazing experience, but the point here that I am making is that while I go on my journey in my being-ness, I affect your ability to find your connection.

And so I ask you to try something a little different. And, I ask that you take your moment of stillness in a room beyond mine, in a space that is clear of my energy and the energy of others, so that you may be among your energy and your connection to the divine, so that you may find within you these multi-dimensional portals that exist within all beings.

Now, it is much easier for me, for I am already detached from logic, and, that is what the human being struggles with, this connection, this deeply felt need to have such a logical interpretation of life. People cannot find their way to the understanding that knows that logic is separating us from the wisdom that exists within our knowingness. And so we, as human beings, go through these challenging efforts to quiet the mind, the mind that we have stirred for centuries with intellectualizations, the mind that we have limited by our false understandings.

And so, my dear, look at this as my way of assisting you in moving more deeply into your own awareness so that yours is not clouded by mine. And although I have said that we are one in this moment as we exist here on the earth plane, we funnel the energy of the divine through these individual perceptive states of being. And so I ask you to find your way through your individual perceptions to your higher self so that we can meet there in the ethers among the energy of our truth.

Tara expresses her gratitude for Peter's guidance, and she declares her intention to continue to expand her connection to her higher self in the energy.

Peter: I do value all of the efforts you have made, and want you to know that there is a sense that there is a shift, and you are becoming more and more available to the interactions between us energetically. And I want to make sure to tell you this so that you may know that it is not that what you are doing is not working, but rather there is a more amenable energy to commence in.

That being said, I also want to bring to your attention this idea that I am using this illness to take my leave, for I do not feel that I can maneuver this physical experience much longer. But, there is also a sense that this is not the end of the journey for us, but, rather, a new beginning, one that will define a new, more expansive co-creative manifestation of the cumulative benefits of our shared journeys. Here my words, dear love, of this and many lives. I am in this one with you fully, regardless of how it looks in the physical, and everything you feel, I feel with you. And so, begin to feel, intuitively, my excitement about our newfound connection and the future, for its expansion is inevitable, and our willingness to be this for one another is timeless. So, you may always know that it is irrelevant what form you exist in, I'm always a part of you, and will always be a part of this experience with you until you, my dear, meet me on the higher realms and we decide together what it is we will journey into together.

I look to shift this doctor [laughter] and his idea of what medicine is for, and how the healing process truly works; for I am about to shift into a new state of awareness, one that is going to move many into new states of understanding. I can leave you with this. There is a sense here that, although it looks as though I am on my last days, it may be longer, for I have some reserve within me that I am looking to bring forward to baffle the medical community. It's a trial run, my dear, it's a trial run, and I am taking it on a daily basis. I will give you that, and I will let you know that it is a matter of time. I am not saying that I am coming back to life as the human being I was in my mid-thirties, but I will say that I am exploring the other side more and more.

As I take my leave into my dream state, I do take my leave of the body. I explore the great beyond, and I am finding more and more comfort there. So I am preparing you, my dear, that I am looking to take this leave, just not in this exact moment. It is coming, it is coming soon, and I have crossed a certain bridge here that I feel will bring me to the confluence of awareness that I am looking for before I leave this earth plane.

And so, it is truly an exploration for I am now pioneering, I am pioneering to the unknown, the unknown that is becoming more and more known in every moment to me. I am aware that there are others here waiting for me, and I don't mean waiting impatiently in any manner at all, but, rather graciously; allowing me to understand that that is who I am, where they are. And, that as I take these sojourns into the depths of my being-ness, I find that these others that were so familiar to me in this life (and in other lives), remind me of who I am and how I fit into where they are. I see it now, almost like a puzzle, a grand and glorious puzzle of life, and I am a certain dimension that will fit only in one precise space saved exactly for me. And for this, I will tell you that there is a space directly in mine that is yours. And yes, we do, we do fit into one another's space quite nicely.

It is something when we actually pull back from it and see how many of us fit into that same space, all together. We don't recognize it or realize it when we're there in the physical. But the layers of self are more readily understood now, as the individuals on the earth plane that we have interacted with, where they are each another layer of us, of we, of the one that we are.

That is what I am learning in my exploration of self. That is where I go in the deeper sleeps that you have seen me take; and so you know. As you look at my body and wonder where is he off to, now you know. I am finding my space in the great beyond so that when it is my time to leave, I can just take a step to the side and know I am stepping into my space.

Laura and Tara express their joy in visualizing an image of the great and beautiful way Peter describes this puzzle interpretation.

Laura: Do you have other questions for Peter?

Tara discusses Peter's care and asks him if she is meeting his needs with all the love and support that comes from her heart.

Peter: I feel as though you are honoring what it is I would wish for. And, although I, as the man that I am, would like that you be relieved of these duties, I also know that there is no other in this world that I would rather be here with me through this than you. You have a way of complementing my energy, and, everything you do makes me feel more complete. So, I say to you, my dear, let yourself know that everything and anything that you do for me is exactly what I need in the moment; for you are the receiver for my inclinations, and you do honor them. Although, in moments you do feel yourself fighting with your own human desires and inclinations, you always pull back, you always pull back to the souls that we are and allow that truth to come forward. So I would say to you, yes, my dear, you are giving me all that I need and more.

And I, as the loving man that I am, want to thank you and give you my eternal gratitude and ask that you take time for you, my dear. You take time to find a moment of joy here and there, for when you do, I feel it. And I want to know that your life has joy, and that it is not all about our journey, but that you can have experiences of your own that bring you joy, that bring you peace, that allow you to recognize the beauty all around us.

Tara: Thank you, my darling. I'm enormously thankful for the eternal love we share.

[End of session/tape.]

Chapter 15

Hark Back

At this time in our grand journey, I had to remind myself that my time with Peter here on Earth was short. Harking back, I could see how dramatically the body, mind and ego were transcended by his soul and his ability to incisively communicate with me.

In the passage of time since our last channeling session on May 15, 2013, my days and nights have been touched by intense yielding to the unavoidable sadness echoed in my heart; reminding me that it is also time for me to prepare for *my* transition. Although my transition will be different than Peter's transition, it is a passage from the life I have been living for nearly ten years. While weeping in private as the off-casting of my tears flowed from my emotional wounds, my capacity to respond with the higher emotions was challenged.

As Peter was preparing for his transition in the face of devastating signs of physical deterioration, even greater significant changes had been occurring. Although I knew that the death of the body was not the end of life, in defiance of the logical understanding of how the human being moves through this process, I still needed to remind myself that we are created of something independent of the flesh — a soul; a timeless spirit and our counterpart that never leaves us.

It is a tribute to Peter and an expression of his conviction that the element that distinguishes contrasting forms is so great and ever so present that it became manifest to my mind and eyes. It is an admission of truth, based on the evidence that may or may not be factually valid for others. And, wow … his ongoing conscious journey to the spirit realm was marked by his amazing ability to conquer fear and courageously experience his transition each step of the way.

Through the courtesy of the following two recorded channeled conversations with Peter, it becomes even more apparent that when a soul is preparing to release the body, the soul continues to thrive. I am so grateful that we had this precious time together, not only to hear him speak to me from his soul while preparing to leave the human experience but to lovingly give him an opportunity to express his self, prior to transitioning to the spirit world.

We are blessed by our faith in the unquenchable light of the spirit.

Chapter 16

Seventh Exchange

(Approximately One Month before Peter's Transition)
Transcript of October 5, 2013
Channeled by Laura Mirante, Channel/Medium

Tara: Peter, I am blessed and so grateful to be here in this exchange with you. I have a sense that you are willing to join me in this physical experience as I create an open space for you. I love you deeply and wish to hear you speak to me again.

Peter, I would like to know about your journey of self-exploration, which we have talked about in our previous channel, and how it affects our smooth, fearless transition into an energy as one.

The following channeled transcription was
recorded and transcribed verbatim:

Peter: Let's begin with this idea of this life being a journey of self-exploration. I do not want to limit it to me and *my* journey, dear one. You know this is our journey, a journey of exploration that *we* are taking together, where we are exploring our individual natures and our collective assumptions. We have so many invested energies together that there is no point where it is obvious that this is where I begin, this where you end, and this is where I am only me. I don't see it that way at

all anymore. I see us as *us*. I see us as moving through this experience with simultaneous movements and in conjunction with simultaneous inclinations of the mind. I do not want to say *thoughts* because that brings us too far into the physical, logical idea of thinking and communicating. I want to say inclinations of the mind, the body-mind, the bigger mind, the higher mind; however it is you want to term that. It's the mind that connects us to one another.

It's the energy where our intuition can flow from one another, where our communication can move between our energies. That's what I see us doing together; investing this lifetime, investing this physical experience in this way so that we can know ourselves as souls on a much deeper level of consciousness, where we can take our surface reality and begin to integrate this imaginary energy of divinity that we exist in.

It's how we see it as human beings, you know ... we see ourselves as existing in an energy of divinity, not that we *are* the energy of divinity. And that's what we are beginning to come to terms with within ourselves, within our connection to one another, that we are not existing in the energy but rather we *are* the energy. We are the energy together. Not that we are two separate energies that need to find a place to commune, but rather the more and more we go through this experience, the more and more we recognize that we flow through one another; that there is no sense that you have to search outside of yourself for me. For now, I feel that you are becoming accustomed to searching within your own sense of knowing from my response to your questions. I see that; I see how you dabble in this process of cross-dimensional communication. I see you reaching for me within your own sense of knowing, and it is a gift.

It truly is a gift to know that you see me beyond the physical body, for that's what you do each time you search your own intuitive sense of knowing from my inclination. You are affording me the possibility that I can reach through the energy that connects us and speak directly to your soul. I see you in your physicality, looking to break the limits of the physical nature. And I must say that I honor you, for I do not know if our positions were reversed if I could do the same for you. And so I have to give you that limitless sense of gratitude that I feel for you, for I know now the beauty and integrity in making this effort and the gift that it is to me. I see it as a gift to you as well, but I can only rectify in me how affecting it is for you to see me beyond my physical body.

I cannot explain to you enough how affecting it is to be seen. It's something so magnificent that I feel as if I want to say that I will be indebted to you forever. But, my darling, I already am, and I wouldn't say in your debt; I just already am yours. And there is no need to feel in debt, for you know that in a different situation, in a different lifetime, I may find it in me to give you this same gift. And I hope someday, some lifetime, that I will be able to offer you this same experience, for it is something to behold. It is something to experience as a human being and as a soul.

It really is quite illuminating to be here in this physical world and not have to be attached to the limitations of the structure of the current society. The more I revel in my divinity, the more I realize the restrictive nature of the current logistics of society and of what is expected of the human being. It really is so far from what our true nature is. It is difficult to appreciate how it is human beings are living now, although I can.

I have been taken into the realms of awareness that see beyond the limitations of fear and anger, lack and insecurity. I have been set free from that, dear one. I want you to know that that is another gift of this experience I am having, that I no longer need to be overwhelmed in stress and anxiety or fear, that which so many others on the Earth are dealing with. I do not have to.

And I am sorry if you feel that you have taken on that responsibility for both of us. I truly wish I could alleviate you of that burden. And I hear you, I hear you saying that it's all just fine and that I've done enough for you in our life together to feel entitled to receive in this way. I know that you feel this way, dear one, and I love you for that. I just, still as the man that I am, want to be the one taking care of you, you know. I feel a simple-minded interpretation of who I am as a man limits me in this way. So I won't stay there, but I did want to give you that sense that I do truly appreciate everything that you are doing for me. And I honor you for doing it in a way that you are, because you are adding a sense of integrity to the experience that most couldn't.

There just isn't a big enough word to thank you for what you're doing for us as the souls that we are. It truly is a grand revelation that you are bringing us through. And it will stay with us, dear one; it will stay with us beyond this lifetime. We will not forget what we learned here. We may temporarily confuse ourselves with it, but we will always come back to this sense of knowing that there is no separation. Regardless of what it appears to be like in the physical, there is no moment in time where you and I are not connected on a soulful level, and, where we are not able to communicate within our own being-ness. That's how I see my journey of self-exploration. Ah, it has brought me back to you and our connection.

Laura: I have to pause here, Tara. That's one of the most beautiful statements that has ever come out of my mouth. It's so beautiful. It's so big as far as the love … it's too big for my heart. It's so big, and so beautiful, and so profound.

Tara: I'm spellbound … [pause] it's a lot for me to take in. I think you have said it for me, Laura, and I thank you.

Peter, I honor you and our journey as eternal souls. The gift of seeing you beyond your physicality *is* magnificent, and it is so easy for me to see you in this way. You have made it possible for me to reach for you. I love you eternally.

Peter: As for the energy that I am exploring, I must say … ah … that we are an intricately created schematic of energetic gridlines that is so developed, so acute, and so intricate that it is difficult to follow a thread. For what happens is I pull on one … I pull on a thread of truth to see where it will lead me, and what happens is it starts moving in a certain direction in this life and takes me to certain experiences that I have had. And then what occurs is I get shifted. I jump threads if you will. And I end up in a totally different aspect of who I am, looking at a totally different emotion and a totally different perception of life that has triggered this emotion. And I am then taken to life experiences that are attached to that thread of truth, and I move through them for a while until once again it appears as though I have jumped the thread. And I begin again on an all-new terrain, an all-new aspect of who I am, and I begin to explore that thread of truth.

It's really quite fascinating to see how the larger mind, the more advanced mental aspect of who we are, knows not to let us stay too long in certain investigatory aspects of this process. We are brought here and there and back and forth, and what I am

beginning to see is a weave coming together — a weave of a new understanding of who I am and what I am capable of. It is as if each time I pull on a thread of truth, I get a bit of integrity that has been established because of the experience that was spurred by that thread of truth in my experiences. And I hold on to that, and I take that, and I weave it into the others that I accumulate as I go through this process. What I see is that the weave is such ... like a basket weave where it won't hold water. And what I mean when I say that, is it will never be complete. It will never be to the point where I feel like I have completed it.

And there is a purpose to that. That *is* the life experience, the physical world experience, the journey of the soul. It is an ever-engaging process of self-evaluation that comes from the efforts at self-exploration. And in the evaluation process, there is no gradation of accuracy. It is not about whether we got it right or wrong; I will tell you that. It is a matter of the intensity with which we engage the experience. And what does that mean to you, the human being? What does it mean when I say the intensity we use to engage the experience? It is about, o-o-h ... oh, it is about how much of our energy we are willing to invest in an experience that is soulfully driven, and, how much of that effort we will use at moving through the process completely to the point of fulfillment of the obligatory energy of resolution we set out to achieve.

Again, don't misinterpret the word *resolution*. It is not that we go through experiences in our lifetime that are problems that we have to fix. I don't mean it in that way at all. The resolution comes within our own sense of knowing who we are and how we are capable of being when placed in a human, physical world situation.

I must remind you that it is never about right and wrong. It is always about intensity, frequency, and how we affect those in our experience, and how they affect our ability at remaining in the frequency we intend on expressing here as the individual aspects of the one we came to be. You know it comes back to recognizing that we are here for the collective experience, through the individual experience; where the individual experience is a means to the collective experience. And what I see now is the human beings get so lost in their individuality, in their sense of individual importance, that they have forgotten that it is only important to the point that it affects the collective.

So, I can say to you, that this journey of self-exploration has really broadened my awareness of how interconnected all life experiences are — and I mean each and every individual on Earth has an effect on each and every individual on Earth.

So you cannot fathom it when you sit there in your body, or I sit there in my body. I've watched the television, and I see those in other countries that are suffering. I cannot fathom this idea that their suffering is moving through my field and affecting me in some way. Yes, I know we've both had our moments where we would feel our heart bleeding for those in other countries and what they're going through, or, even at a time for those in our country and what they have experienced. But it's much more than that; it's much more than just a feeling of compassion or empathy that you can recognize logically. It's so much more, so much more than that. I cannot even come up with the kind of metaphor that I can use to even give you a sense of how affecting we are to one another while we are here in the physical, and even when we are not.

And that's the other thing, you know; I get visits, I get visits now. I get visits quite regularly from our loved ones on the other side. They do come to give me a sense of our connection, and they do come to give me a sense of their support for my journey; and they offer me information regarding the experience on a much more expansive level. They have given me insights, such as what I am giving you today, so that I can be here, on the earth plane, in the body with the expansive awareness that most only receive when they leave the body.

Again, it is this "illness" that has afforded me this opportunity to bridge the gap between worlds in our mind. I must say that as a logically driven human being, I never could have imagined that this is what this kind of experience brings to a human being. It's so interesting to think of how we look from the outside at a person having an experience such as what I am having. And we look at them with sadness, with a sense of limitation being placed on their experience; and meanwhile, look at the expansive nature of the experience that we are having. Think about the gifts that keep coming as a result of this experience. And then ask yourself if you could ever look at another in my similar situation with any sense of apathy or sadness on their part that they have been denied a certain physical-world experience. Can you see now the absolute redundancy in that thought? ... to know that here I am as the soul that I am, having one of the most magnificent experiences of my life while not fully engaging the physical world.

It really is quite something to integrate into our logical understanding of who we are, and so I say to you, humbly and in great awe, thank you. Thank you so much for being willing to hear this from me, to know me in this way, and to honor our journey as souls together, for that is what you've done. You have fought the logical mind's inclination to play that role of victim to the illness. You have not allowed either myself or yourself to go to that state of apathetic behavior. And, I will say one more time, that in this lifetime as a man that I was, I do not know that I would have had the same courage as you, or the same wherewithal to follow through on the intuitions that got you here to this point, to this kind of communication with Sally* and now with Laura.

I know, that you did recognize that there were so many different signals moving you in this direction, and, that it was inevitable because our souls would not have let us go through this experience without recognizing and realizing that this was possible. It truly is the defining point on our journey together. And although we've had many wonderful physical world experiences, this is what we will truly take away when we leave our physical bodies. It will be the realizations that have brought us closer together, the real efforts that were made by both of us to initiate more movement between us energetically than ever before. So again, I congratulate you; I congratulate you on breaking through the limiting belief systems and allowing yourself to recognize me in you. I feel that that's where you are at this point, where you are truly beginning to see me in a more obvious way where it's not so uncertain anymore. I do not feel the same hesitation that I once did in your ability to believe what I was imparting to you energetically. I feel you now responding energetically back to me.

And so, I would say to you — as you ask me, how is my journey of self-exploration going — I ask you the same thing. I see you moving through it yourself in your own way on this level of consciousness, as I move through it on my level of consciousness. And as we bring those levels of consciousness closer and closer together, we are recognizing each other in different ways now. It is wonderful to know that we can do this together. It is wonderful to know that we have a partnership in this and that we are really expanding into something magnificent together.

It will be quite different for you when I do take my leave than for most others that you know in this life that have lost a partner. For you will know that you will not have lost me. For you will feel me. You will be with me as I take that leap of consciousness. You are going to feel me shifting in you. And, you are going to realize that it is time for you to get ready to expand even more in order to allow me to come through even clearer than I did when I was here in your physical presence. I believe that to be true, Tara. I believe that when I leave this body, you'll be able to hear me clearer.

I think there are still some hesitations in me that affect the clarity of our communications. And isn't that quite interesting coming from my soul [laughter], in this moment, to know that although I may appear detached from the physical world and the logical mind, I still ... ah, I still feel affected by it. I still feel some of the limiting belief systems surfacing at times in my mind. And although there is always a divine response that surfaces as well from within my soul, I still find myself contemplating the logical interpretation of it all. And, isn't that quite interesting to know that that is what is occurring in me at times, that I feel the divinity in connecting as we do intuitively, and then I think, *how could I have just said that to her when I can't properly communicate what it is I am thinking and feeling?* And I have those conscious thoughts, those conscious moments of awareness of how did that happen. But they don't last, and I float right back into that ethereal sense of knowing. And so I find it interesting in my state that I can have that kind of back-and-forth in me.

**And, I think about you and all other human beings that have
that logical mind running full force, at full capacity, twenty-four
hours a day, seven days a week and think,** *how could you ever find
the moments of stillness, quiet the mind long enough to hear me?*
**And when I think about that … ah … I think about how much
you truly love me, to devote this time in your life to this kind of
journey of self-exploration, so that we can still know each other,
and so that we could still see each other as the loving beings of
life that we are.**

[Pause here.]

Laura: Do you have anything to add here or any questions?

Tara: I just want to say how deeply moved I am by Peter's words.
[Pause here.]

Laura: I feel there is something here Peter wants to talk about,
but I don't know what it is. Is there any situation that is going on at
home that you want to ask Peter about?
[Pause here.]

Tara: Yes. There *is* a person he will want to talk about. We had
a visitor who spent time with Peter, and each morning for thirty to
forty-five minutes, she massaged his hands and feet and played some
of his favorite classical music. I want to know how he felt about her.
Laura: Yes! Yes! That's who he wants to talk to you about!
Peter: As far as [Name omitted to grant anonymity.] **is concerned,
I would say that she helped us both shift to the next level. She
really instigated some movements in me energetically, regardless
of whether she was aware of it or not. I do feel that there was
a significant shift in both of us because of her presence in our**

experience. It really goes back to what I was saying about how interesting it is to see how we affect one another. And what I would say is that we are not the only ones shifted by the experience; that she herself left a different person than when she came.

For her, I am letting myself begin to be open to a more gentle side of me. I have begun to open up to the soft underbelly beneath the surface of my manhood. I would say that I am moving more fully into the area of myself that is directed by the feminine energy more than the masculine. And I do not mean to imply anything in the physical; I am just saying that what I have explored regarding our nature is that we are both masculine and feminine in form. Some have more masculine than feminine, and others have more feminine than masculine, and, it is not necessarily connected to the gender.

I will say that it's more about the energetic makeup we are as souls. And what I see now is that I have a dramatic feminine side to my field that I did not allow to fully manifest in this physical lifetime. I see that there is something in her that instigated this area of exploration in me, and that she herself has felt some connection to that aspect of me. And, in her instigating in me the awakening, it shifted something in her, where the feminine energy moving through me, moved through her, and shifted into her a sense of her entitlement to act, in this life, from that creative aspect of who she is. She left us, feeling freer than she had allowed herself to be previously.

And, I would say that it's interesting for me to have this kind of insight on another in the physical world, as I sit here in my still place and commune only on the energetic levels of consciousness. Ah, another unfolding of truth before us that, as one engages me in a selfless manner in the situation that I am in, they tap into an area of truth in them that changes everything in their perception of their life. And so it will be interesting to see what occurs over the coming months as others come forth to engage me now.

Tara: What a fascinating experience that was!

Peter, I'd like to know if your digestive system has improved since I've changed your meals to more holistic and alkaline-based foods?

Peter: A lot of relief; that's what I want to bring forward first. I feel a significant shift in my digestive system, and I feel — I feel less bloated. I feel less inflamed on the inside; that's what I want to say. Much of the medication had really interrupted the digestive flow within me, and that what you are doing is reestablishing a balance in my digestive system. Although there's more to it than that, what I see is that it affects every area of my health. There is so much more to the digestive system than just the digestive system; that it really is affecting every different organ in many different ways. So I would say that overall, you have created a significant shift in the balance of my internal makeup and that that itself is another beautiful gift that you are giving to me.

I don't see that there's anything missing in my diet; I will say that. I don't feel that I am limited in any way, and I do feel that nutritionally I am getting all of the benefits of the energy of the food that I can. The most important thing is that it's real, that it's real food that my body can really work with, and that's what I am most grateful for.

Tara: Peter, I'm so happy to hear this. Can you also address the issue about what seems to be some discomfort with your teeth and mouth?

Peter: Very clear; it is a matter of bacteria. It is not your fault; there's nothing you could do to prevent it. It simply is a part of this process. It is a redundancy. It is as if the digestive

system is working overtime to create the balance and overwhelm the inflammation within the system that it is creating almost an acidic environment in the mouth. And I do not want you to shift the diet because of the benefits it is having to my digestive system. And it's interesting to see this dichotomy within the body for you would think that if ...

[End of session/ tape.]

Tara: The time spent with Peter is never long enough, and when a tape stops recording abruptly and before Peter finishes speaking (as was the case here); it is very disappointing. Nevertheless, I wish to say that the portion missed was essentially the following: *Peter suggested that I add aloe vera to his diet for its healing properties and benefits to the digestive system.*

Chapter 17

Eighth Exchange

(One Day before Peter's Transition)
Transcript of November 1, 2013
Channeled by Laura Mirante, Channel/Medium

Tara: Peter, I feel you deeply at this time, and I wish I could ease the current emotional instability sensed in my heart as the signs of our transition are eminently felt. I've been moved to arrange this channeled session for I wish to commune with you for support, and to give you an opportunity to reach me. Inasmuch as we have prepared for very precious moments such as this, it is taking everything I have deep in my heart and soul to move into our state of transition. I feel that you are bravely and lovingly prepared and I am deeply grateful for this.

Tara offers Peter the platform.

> *The following channeled transcription was*
> *recorded and transcribed verbatim:*

Peter: Clearly, my love, I have made an impact on both of our understandings of what it is to be physical, what it is to be a soul, and what it means to move more fully into the "all that is." And, as I have taken my time moving into this expanse that we are, I am coming to the realization that there is no separation at

all, that I myself will blink, and in an instant I will be released from the dense environment of the physical body. And I will feel lighter, more free, more expansive than I could possibly hope to achieve in this physical body. And so I say to you, my dear, I am, in this moment, at the precipice of limitless awareness, and I realize the immensity of this motion I am making. And although I have been in this condition for some time, I feel it as if it were new now. I feel it as if I just stepped into this expression of self that is so detached from the physical that it appears as if I've already dismissed my physicality.

And yet, I will say to you, with all that I am that I am fully present in this moment with you. I am here, and I am available to you in the energy. I am embracing you already energetically. And I feel that you are inspired by my willingness to hold true to all that I have been to you. And that I will, in this moment, let you have a sense of me as I make my transition. I feel as though we are ready to take this next step together, and that I have experienced all that I wish to experience here in the physical in this kind of circumstance.

Dear one, I extend myself to you as you move through this moment of transition, for I hope that you, my dear, will realize that you too are in a moment of transition. It is not only I that transitions. My transition may be more recognizable because of the release of my physicality, but in truth, dear one, you are transitioning into a new, more expansive aspect of you as well. And so together we leap forward into this limitless awareness and see what it is we can create from the understanding we have of each other and the connection we have strengthened through these last few years.

It is so different than how most people would experience our kind of situation. And isn't it something to think that although most fear the kind of conditions we had to work under, we embraced them and grew because of that. We allowed each other to experience the moment in whatever way we felt was appropriate, in that moment. I did not put conditions on you, as you did not put conditions on me. And that, my dear, is how we were able to move through this seemingly limited condition with an awareness that this was exactly what we were to use to set us off on a new path; to give us a sense of a new journey and a new purpose in our coming together in this lifetime.

Finding my way to you was as simple as opening my eyes. I felt, from the moment I was born, I was meant to be with you, and I knew that my search would continue until I had you in my arms. And so I know it will be for us in the future. I know that we will traverse many incarnations together and that we will once again find our way to each other in the physical. Although we may look different, we will recognize our energies. We will recognize our connection, and we will feel that deep sense of knowing that surfaces when two souls come together in the physical. I give you this, for I see it already. I see it in our future and I know it to be true. And, I want you to realize that this is the game of life, and this is how we play; you and I, back and forth, from lifetime to lifetime, finding each other, experiencing life together, and growing together from our experiences.

And this is one of them. This is one of the most productive and rewarding life experiences in the physical that we have come together and appreciated as one. And this, I can say, is because of your willingness, dear one, your willingness to step outside of the linear interpretation of my situation. If it weren't for your willingness and our dear friend, Beverly Dowdle [She introduced us to channeling.], we could not have shifted our conscious understanding of what it was we were doing.

And so, as I have said before, I will be eternally grateful for your strength, your integrity, and your devotion to our commitment together. It truly is what defines you, my love. It truly is how I see you, as that commitment that kept me going, that inspirational energy that allowed me to experience newness in my life right up to the very end. There are no words for the kind of opportunity you gave me; for the gratitude I feel for your ability to rise above the fear to question each and every intellectual interpretation of who I was, until you found the interpretation that felt right at the deepest part of your core. There in the center of your truth we met again, and it is there that I will exist as a part of your experience until we meet in spirit as one.

I give you all that I have to give. I extend to you now my awareness, the awareness I've accumulated in this lifetime. I give it to you as a gift from me. I give you the ability to tap into all that I am, all that I know, and all that I ever will be. For I know that you will continue to strengthen our connection regardless of where I am perceiving life from.

I acknowledge that as I move through this transition and you sit in stillness, you will feel yourself as a part of my transition as you open up your heart and let our love flow. It will lead you to me, to the aspect of me that is free. And you will feel it, and you will know it, and you will honor all that you did for me and all that you did for us as the united energy of truth, love, and integrity.

We did it, my dear, what no other human being has been capable of doing. We have experienced life together. We have allowed each other to delve deep into the core of our being-ness and find our true soulful connection. And, through that connection, you have been able to know what it is I was experiencing, even though I could not speak, even though I could not give you a sense of the joining I was a part of. Your willingness to reach beyond the logical understanding of what I was experiencing was what allowed us to create that bridge, that bridge that will continue on, that bridge that will allow us to continue to communicate.

The thing I want to bring up here is it will become easier for you once I have left my physicality. The stress, the worry, the support for my physicality will be released. There will be none of that for you to engage in. And as you move through the grieving process — which, my dear, I want you to know I wholeheartedly embrace — I do not expect you to not grieve my physicality. I know you may feel as though there is pressure because of your understanding of our connection and our continuity, but I honor the idea that I, the man that you knew so well, loved so well, trusted so well and shared your life with, will no longer be here in the physical for you to see, hear, and touch. And I embrace the idea that we are human beings and as a part of that physical experience, there will be those moments of grief, and I want you to allow yourself to have them.

It does not mean you don't honor me as a soul; it does not mean you don't recognize our connection. It only expresses the emotions that are stirred up when two that have such a strong bond together begin to shift into different ways of experiencing this life. That's how I want you to see it, my dear. Not that I've left, not that you've lost me, but that I've shifted into a different way of experiencing life.

If you could, imagine that I've moved across the globe, and I exist in a country far from your reach, but that we can still communicate over the Internet. If you could just put that image into your mind, as a means to define for the mind what is occurring, it is a much more expansive image than that of my body in ashes, or beneath the ground. Continue to see me as a part of your existence, just with a little more distance between us. And so, you know if I moved away you would be sad, and I would honor that sadness because it is your truth. So in your moments of missing me, I will be there, holding your hand and letting you know that it is only temporary.

And when you find your way out of the sadness, you will know that I will be there in the most demonstrative way that I can so that you will recognize me. From what I understand, it is more difficult for a human being in grief to elevate to the frequency that we can connect. But, I know that that does not stand true for you, that your moments of grief will be that. There will be moments defined by grief that you move through and let go of; and that you will define your life more by our newfound purpose, our purpose of strengthening this connection we have created to the point where you will feel me. You will know me, and you will hear me more than you have in these past few years.

As the grief begins to lift and life begins to fall into place for you, you will find those moments of freedom from fear, freedom from the sadness and the idea that I am gone. And, you will find me creating new adventures for us to take, where it is as if I instigate movements or a sense of the direction in you, and you feel inspired to take that signal and to create your experience around it.

I do realize that I have more of my own processing to go through as I make my transition, but it does not mean that I cannot be a part of your experience as well. The more I traverse the great ravine, the more I recognize how multifaceted we are, how many aspects of me are available to me, where I can be in one moment with you, and in the same moment, having an experience in my awareness, processing my life.

It's not going to be like many have defined the transitional process. For me, it is going to be at rapid speed that I move through my reevaluation process, for I have done so much of it here in the physical while I was detached from all of the nonsense of the physical world. And, so, it will be a new experience for me as the soul that I am, as well, for I have never experienced a transition such as this — this beautiful gift you've given me, honoring my soul in the way in which you did, the way in which you do.

I ask that you share this experience with many, so that others may realize what is going on within the minds of their loved ones, within the souls of their companions and parents. There are many that would benefit from the understanding you have achieved of who we are as souls, and many that would be thrilled to know that their loved ones are in there, and that their souls are experiencing an expanse like nothing they could have hoped for. We have so much to share and so many to affect with and through this experience, my dear. I hope you find that kind of inner strength, determination and focus to allow our journey to be shared, and to extend the kind of opened-hearted acceptance to any and all that look for support from you as they move through a situation similar to ours.

You're a much stronger human being than I ever could have been, my dear. You have proven it over and over, again and again, and I stand here now in awe of the dignity with which you moved through each experience. And I know, beyond all doubt, that our experience, as defined by our souls, was fully represented in this lifetime; that there is not one inkling of regret in either of our soulful perceptions of our human lives.

Master the intelligent mind, my dear. Put it in its place and let it realize it is the supporter of the soul, that the intellectual mind is only there to follow the whim and will of the higher self.

Let yourself feel entitled to move away from those in our experience that would have you living a different kind of life. And there will be those judging what it is you put your energy into now and how it is you look to exist here now. Many will have a say; many will have an opinion; many will give you their opinions of what they think is best for you. But how many can know you the way that I do? How many can know all that you have been through, all that we have been through, and the kind of awareness that you have now? My only regret is to leave you with no one in our experience that knows the depth of our connection. You must be willing to share these experiences with others, for many reasons, my dear, for many reasons. Of course, there is the profound effect these kinds of exchanges will have on those that are open enough to hear them; but, more than this, so that you can find the ones that can support you in this kind of journey, that can give you this same kind of purpose that I do in communicating energetically.

You're going to want to realign your life now, my dear. Do not feel that you have to hold on to any of the old. Do not feel that you have to hold on to any of the past, for it is already embedded in our being-ness. Each and every experience we have exists in our fields and always will. So you do not have to hold on to the stuff to remember our experiences — they are a part of you, as they are a part of me.

And, although it may console you for some time, you will know when it is time to release yourself from the home we shared, for I feel that you will want to stay in it, as you feel that it is filled with my energy. And that may be true for some time, but there will come a point where I expand into the all that is beyond the limitations of this current life persona. And it is at that point you will know, you will know that my energy is now beyond limitation, no longer feeling any attachment to anything in the physical. The only connection I will have — and I will not call it an attachment — is a connection that exists between you and me; and that you can take anywhere you go, my dear. I exist within you. I will exist because of you. I know that you recognize this, and I know that you and I will have many opportunities to share joyous exchanges together again, in this life.

You will find my humor a little less rigid as I move more and more away from my body, mind, and ego. I feel a lightness. I feel a deeper connection to joy than I have ever felt, and I am realizing that that is what I am moving into, the joy of life, the joy of existing as energy in a physical body. It is true bliss, my dear, true bliss that I am moving into, that I am becoming a part of.

There is no sense of separation. There is no sense of any need for me to detach from the physical, for I feel that I have already done that. And as I step more fully into my being-ness, I will leave this body without any incident, without any recognition that I am no longer a part of that. As I speak in this moment, I am unsure if I *am* a part of it. That is how I feel, as if I have already taken my leave. I feel as if I am already speaking to you, from the great beyond, [Laura: There is a bit of humor in the way he said that.] and yet, I know that I am still there, that there is a part of me still holding on to that last little connection I have to the body, mind, and ego.

I am still having my fun with the medical community though, aren't I? I can't say that I am going to completely shock the medical community this time, but I am making it quite difficult for them to predict my movements, aren't I? And I do enjoy that. I do enjoy feeling as if I am the one in control, and isn't that another gift I get to give to you? Another gift to show you how powerful our souls are, regardless of what it is we think logically is occurring medically, scientifically. It is all irrelevant when it comes to our soul's desire. And, in this moment, I do look to extend to you a sense that I am not going to draw this out. I am not going to make this more difficult than it has to be. But I want you to recognize that I am just having a little fun, and I hope you can join me in that. I do love to see the faces as they try to contemplate what to tell you.

Tara and Laura assure Peter that they are enjoying this as well.

Tara: Peter, how do you see your legacy?

Peter: Ah, my dear, I have already addressed this. I want to be remembered, as the soul that would not give up on his human counterpart. And I want you to be seen as the human that would not give up on her soulful counterpart. And I want people to know that it did not matter what perceptive state of being we were in, but that we could communicate, and we could have and share this experience together. I think it's the most important thing either of us has ever experienced in our life. And if we are to grow as a soulful community, then we must share our most expansive blessings. And this, my dear, is how I intend to live on in the physical — through you, through your words that you share with others in expressing this divine commitment that we have had to one another, and that we will still engage regardless of my form.

I do not want to dismiss the idea that you are now going to be free to find a life that sustains you, a life that fills you, body, mind, and soul. But I do want to impress on you the importance of this experience we shared together and how it can impact others. I want you to recognize that there is much for you to share, and there is so much for people to know about our soulful connection. And although you have never been one to put yourself out in front as far as our joint ventures are concerned, you must recognize that this is your time to shine. This is your time to be in the limelight, and that I am the one now to be the supporter of your experience, that I am only here to assist you now on your physical journey. And through that willingness, we both expand as the souls that we are.

I cannot express enough the kind of immense gratitude I feel for your ability to remain so open and so connected, regardless of the uncertain state of emotions that you feel in the moment-by-moment basis. I feel that, you know. I feel your emotional instability, and I see how strong you are, regardless of that inclination to just fall prey to the emotion. And I want you to let yourself feel for a while. I want you to fully embrace that process of letting go, and recognize that the grief is a part of that. You must let go of my physicality, for it confines me. It limits my ability to expand into the totality.

[Pause here.]

Tara: Peter, I love you, and thank you for this enlightening exchange. You have a very beautiful way of assisting me in this difficult time.

Are you in any pain and do you need pain medication?

Peter: As I consider this, I must say that I am, in this moment, adjusting to the shift in consciousness I am experiencing. So I am not so focused on the physical pain, although I do see the medication as something that can assist me in the process,

I will say that. So, I am not opposed to it, but I do not want you to think that I am struggling in any way, or that I am experiencing anything beyond my capacity as far as the pain is concerned.

Tara: Peter, please know that I am here in the energy, supporting you at each step of the way. You are the most courageous being I know. It must take a lot to come to this point in your beautiful transition.

Are you in need of any food or drink?

Peter: It is a part of the natural process. I am no longer attached to the body as a soul, so I no longer look to continue to try to have it function in the way that most people see as normal. I'm letting it go, I'm letting it all go, so do not worry about it. I'm not going to suffer for long; I am not going to suffer at all. I'm already experiencing the bliss. So I do not feel that I require anything else from the physical. I almost see the food as a grounding technique, where it was benefiting me as long as I wanted to stay. And I see now that the less I have, the less I ingest, the freer and the lighter that I feel.

Tara: Thank you, Peter. Is there anyone you would like me to call on the phone so they can say their last good-byes to you?

[Pause here.]

Laura [to Tara]: Yeah, Tara, there is somebody, but I don't know how I'm gonna get it, but let me see what we can do.

[Pause here.]

Peter: It is a childhood friend that I long to hear. There was this deep spiritual connection, and I feel that a part of their soul is already experiencing my transition with me.

Laura: Do you have an idea of who this is, Tara?

Tara: Peter, is this person still here or in the spirit world?

Peter: Still alive.

Tara: Peter, is it a boy or girl … a childhood friend?

Peter: Boy.

Tara: Peter, is it someone you were friends with in New York as a little boy 'til the age of two or … I'm not sure at what age you relocated. Or, was it after you moved here to Kentucky?

Peter: New York.

Laura: Tara, you know, that's the kind of connection I felt. It felt really pure, like just a soul kind of … you know what it is. It's like the soul that came in his early childhood to remind him … you know what I mean … to give him that sense that you're not alone here. And so it's kind of interesting that he wants to tap back into that energy cause that's what he said earlier. There was just a deep, spiritual connection between them.

Peter: I am already experiencing the energy, as it is a nonlinear kind of condition, and just by intending to reacquaint me with that energy, I am already making that connection. It's really quite something to see how this all works from my point of view. It's as if our joined intentions allowed me to connect with that soul on a higher frequency. And so I do not want you to overextend yourself in a valiant search, for I do not feel that there is even the time to find that human being and bring him to me. But I realize now that it was never the human being that I needed, just the energy which I am receiving in this moment.

Tara: Peter, it's so touching. It's been a moving experience for me too.

[Pause here.]

Tara: Peter, would you like me to place a call to your daughter, Lisa, and granddaughter, Kelly?

Peter: I would appreciate extending your energy in that direction. I feel that we will all benefit by making that kind of connection, and so I would say, yes. This is an inclination I wish for you to follow, and I do hope it will bring healing for each of us.

Tara: Peter, I will certainly call Lisa and Kelly. I'm sure it will bring healing for all of us.

Peter: I feel that the connection made by your effort will be enough and that we will join energetically, immediately as you do.

There is little left for me to do here, my dear. As you know, we have experienced life to the fullest, and we have experienced so much more than most. And I have allowed myself to let go of what defined my earlier years so that I could have this new life experience with you. And I want you to know there is nothing I am missing; there is nothing I am needing. I feel whole. I feel healthy. And I feel complete in my transition. I feel that all of my needs are being met and that it is just a matter of logistics now.

As you let yourself be taken into the next phase of your journey, know that I follow you; that I extend my energy to you at all times, in all moments, and will never leave your side. I will be a bubble of love around you. That is another image you can have of me, where I am embracing you with all that I am, and I create around you a bubble of protection, a bubble of awareness, and a bubble of love that goes with you always, everywhere.

Together we will traverse this enormous ravine of fear, and we will allow others to know that it is possible to continue life together, regardless of our form or the form that our energy is taking. It is our journey; it is our mission; it is our purpose to be

this for the collective and to be this for each other. And, that is all I need to know … that you have given your life, given everything you are over to this experience for us to have together, for us to appreciate with a much grander understanding of who we are, and for us to share so that others, too, may feel entitled to have this kind of exchange … to have this kind of shift, interpretation of what is occurring.

It is our divine right to exist here in a manner that supports our soul. And we lived true to that, you and I. And we will continue together to experience life in the physical, as two souls committed to one another and devoted to the exploration of self.

I will not say good-bye. I will not say that I am letting you go. I am just shifting, my dear, and you are shifting with me. So let's enjoy this moment of transition and allow life to show us the newness and the brilliance of uncovering truth through each other's experience. Let yourself feel as though this is only the beginning, for that is how I feel. It's the beginning of a new time for us, for a new era for us, for a new phase for us on this journey of self-exploration that we have taken together. So I extend to you my energy as always, my dear, knowing that you will reach out for it and that you will feel my loving embrace always.

Tara: That's *so* beautiful; it's like a *love letter* from heaven. Peter, I love you deeply, and I wish to thank you for all of the magnificent gifts of expansive awareness you have given me in preparation for *my* transition.

Peter: I am beginning to feel quite excited, and I want to share that with you, that what I am experiencing now is not pain but it is …

Tara interrupts: My heart is feeling excitement too, Peter ….

Laura: I know, I know, Tara. And it's just amazing to me that he had to let you know that he's getting excited. G-d bless you; you're an amazing woman. I'm in awe of you.

Tara: Because of you, Laura, Peter and I were able to experience this grand journey together. We can't thank you enough; and Sally* and Beverly.

[Pause here.]

Tara: Laura … is Sally* with Peter now?

Laura: Yes, just a minute. Sally*, please go ahead.

> *Sally*: I have to tell you, my dear friend Tara, that I too am in awe of you. That I am experiencing such a grand exchange of love, integrity, and light because of what it is you two are willing to experience in the physical. I cannot express to you, the gratitude I feel for continuing to move through this experience with such integrity, with such a sense of hope, and such a willingness to know that we are divine, and that we are limitless, and that there is no death. It truly is a testament to what it is I gave my life over to. And so, I will be forever grateful to you, my dear friend, for allowing me to see the benefits of my efforts in the physical.*
>
> *As far as I am concerned, I cannot feel any more excited for the two of you, for I do sense what is coming for the two of you. And I see now how willing you are to experience Peter beyond the physical and how open he is to attempting to bridge the gap in the perception. And so, just know that it is truly something*

to be excited about, this joining that occurs beyond the physical.

As Laura can quite clearly express to you, I never left, I simply stepped to the side, and she simply perceived me in a new way. And there was never a moment where we skipped a beat. There was never a moment where she let herself fall prey to the fear and dismiss my truth. I am grateful for all of you, for the beauty with which you are experiencing life, and I know that my life in the physical had a lot to do with your willingness to be this open and this expansive. And I want you to know that I will never, never leave any of your experiences. I am a part of who you are; I am a part of this experience between Peter and you, Tara. I am a part of it so deeply engrained; I do not see where I end, and Peter begins. I want you to know that, and that is how it is with you and Peter. There is no separation. That is how it is with all of us. There is no separation.

And we have found our way back to our truth, and now we are experiencing life in the physical with that knowingness. There's no greater achievement in humanity than this. So be proud, dear ones, for you are the ones in the physical that are honoring our continuity.

Peter: I just have to mention that I *am* a part of Sally's* energy, I do feel that way, I *do* feel her in my experience. It's such a strange thing to interpret logically, but I am with her more than I am with my physical body. That's what I would say, that she just lifts

me right out of my physicality and lets me know that it's just a step to the side.

Tara: I am eternally grateful for all of us having this beautiful experience. I love you, Peter, and I thank you for sharing your magnificent spirit. I honor you.

[End of session/tape.]

Perhaps you will agree that if there was anyone who did *not* leave anything unsaid before passing, it was my beloved husband, Peter.

Chapter 18

Grief with Gratitude

Like the light of a lighthouse, I radiated my soul light out to Peter as I gave myself over to the glory of the next phase of our journey. On November 2, 2013, Peter made a smooth, fearless, "conscious" transition and arrived at another state of awareness — a divine place of acceptance, love, peace and joy. In all of his magnificence, he manifested his extraordinary journey from the heart of the spiritual being that he truly is. Our divine commitment has made this an unsurpassed journey so far, and our limitless gratitude and love for each other are eternal. Fully understanding the meaning of these essentially wordless revelations is difficult to manage.

I submit to the pulse of my distressing grieving process as I reminisce over the past decade. I now see more clearly how paramount it was to have the proper support Peter needed to go to a new level and meet his spiritual needs, and to lead me to new levels of understanding of "what was underneath." I knew on some level deep within me, that I was meant to do what I did for Peter and for us, by honoring that connection and feeling I not only accomplished it, but that I gave every aspect of myself over to the process. I knew that with every fiber of my being-ness, I would take our energies into a balanced place to feel the love in a given and true way. I chose to stay true, loyal, and present at every turn so that no matter what we needed, I had faith that the universe would be there to provide it.

Memories of the preceding decade and where I am now feel deeply intertwined. I am grateful for the magnificent journey Peter and I created and shared so fully.

At this time I also want to untie the knots of my past so that I can distil the valuable lessons and give the reader a greater understanding of where Peter and I have been and what we have encountered. Untying these knots of memories that were so charged with not only wondrous moments of joy and love, but at the same time with pain, gives me a clearer perspective of my role as wife and caregiver.

I wore the pain of my husband's daily struggle on top of my deep sadness of watching his decline and the conditions marked by fright and peril. I suffered from underlying feelings of mental tension and bodily stress as if my skin stretched tightly inside of me. At times, as I waded gently to calmer waters, these emotions swept through me at a fever pitch as I tried to carry myself with caring and dignity, compassion and forgiveness.

Although I cannot change my past omissions, what I can do is rise to a more divine place and embrace the importance of our profound lessons for the benefit of others experiencing our same situation. Perhaps others will relate to us through the transparent vulnerability exposed by our souls in this process. In the end, our souls knew we had to take these steps to enable us to do what we came here to do.

I have had the unusual opportunity of examining my role in our grand journey by reading through the recorded channeled transcriptions. I realize that I made mistakes treading new waters, sometimes wading gently but not always knowing what to do. Caught up in what the physical demands were, I often wondered — *how do I find a moment to feel who we are on a spiritual level?* So many different kinds of intensities can take over your emotions and your way of dealing with each other. I was tired. Combining the act of what I was doing each day as physical work and my work of the spirit, and feeling both at the same moment was something that did not always resonate within me. Eventually, just being in the moment and realizing there is the spiritual aspect, and there is a give-and-take between our souls was my opportunity to discover the deeper, more wondrous light way to react. With Peter's guidance, tuning-in on a soul-to-soul level expanded my awareness beyond the physical and eventually helped to blend these two experiences, which proved to be a catalyst for our profound transformation.

The day Peter made his transition; I had to take care of things that had to be done while every fiber of my body was fighting against a tide of emotions unfolding before me. I felt trauma; I felt pain. I felt hurt for all of the arduous yet wondrous days and nights throughout the past decade that I had my dear husband in my arms — and now he's gone. I also felt joy for our striving and how we relished our aspirations to continue forward supported by our faith and the beauty of our love.

As I wept, I envisioned my life without Peter and felt frozen in time as the initial emptiness of losing his physicality consumed me. After everyone who had supported me during this day had left, I stood at the bottom of the stairs and watched his body carried on a stretcher, down the stairs and taken away for the last time. He would now, forever be taken from my sight.

My heart was breaking. I felt as though I too was withdrawn into the dimness, and a portion of my heart had given in, with Peter. Shrouded in my tears and overshadowed by the finality of this moment, all of our treasured memories seemed to come again to the surface. I thought about the end days when I cradled and rocked him in my arms as I sang sweetly, softly to him — a hymn called "Veni Creator Spiritus" which I had learned as a little girl in catechism school — a hymn that I had never sung since childhood, until then. It always made me cry. It was so beautiful and a comforter and guide of our hearts. As I stood there alone for the first time, my tears flowed as I now choked on the sounds and sights of what remained behind.

Soon afterward, strength in what remained behind somehow protected my faith that looks through the pain of parting. Although it appeared as if my life would never recover, my instincts told me that the stage was set for the manifestation of our evolution on personal and planetary levels, bringing forth a co-creative dance with life. I knew that the death of the body made way for the everlasting life of the soul. I envisioned our next lifetime together — we would open into divine inspiration and heal in the magic of the vast energetic field. I knew that we would continue together as two souls experiencing life in the physical and devoted to the exploration of ourselves. Just as Peter had told me: "It's the beginning of a new time for us, for a new era for us, for a new phase for us on this journey of self-exploration that we have taken together."

My grief softened by my gratitude, I thought about all the special gifts Peter freely gave to me that will be deeply meaningful to my future. I thought about how he showed me the way to shift into a different experience of life and to taste the joy and richness of our union. I thought about all the sweet and bitter memories embedded in my heart that I am grateful for becoming a part of ourselves. These memories and his gentle soul, beautiful love and energy leave me breathlessly moved. In the most profound source of gratitude in the midst of grief, my pain mitigated.

Gripped by Peter's inimitable courage, integrity, and passion for truth in the pursuit of sharing our extraordinary spiritual journey, I am, in awe. I thank him for showing me how to live a contemplative life, how to feel the wonderment of being real and true to myself, and how to feel the soulfulness that time does not exist. Finding this aspect of myself at play when I am not mindful of time or space, or when I am feeling taken up completely by that energy of spirit is amazing.

With deepest respect, admiration, and with all that I am and will ever be, I honor Peter's soul. I am grateful for the glory of our eternal love, and our grand journey of self-exploration, which taught us more than we ever could have imagined. I thank him for making it possible for me to see him and know him beyond his physicality.

Chapter 19

Bitter/Sweet

Immediately following my husband's passing, I reflected on the overwhelming beauty of our sweet and bitter moments shared over the past decade. I wanted to keep these cherished memories close to my heart and find a way to go there repeatedly, but without the pain. I shed tears often, loudly, and wept softly. I felt regret that my memories could neither be undone nor experienced without pain. The sweet ones were no longer there for me to experience physically, and the bitter ones … too emotionally charged. I just wanted to return to the images of our blissful moments and explore, sense, and reminisce about what now seemed to be all I had left.

The sense of touch was no longer there. The sight of Peter was replaced by forever having to take my eyes off him. As the pain of remembering seemed to fill those voids, I wished to find a way to engage my heart and touch my memories without the pain. I started writing about my memories, one at a time, and I found writing connected everything within me and outside of me. The more I recalled each sweet and bitter moment, the more I was able to grieve and let go of the pain.

As each painful and joyful memory seemed to remind me of the pain and pleasure, sadness and joy, and how disheartening and spirited these emotions can feel, I was free to experience life through new eyes. With memories that now strengthen me, I felt a deep sense of gratitude for having these moments show up on our path as glorious gains with a wider outlook on life and spiritual growth. While looking through the lens of gratitude, the past became a source of joy.

Repeatedly recalling and writing down each bitter/sweet memory allowed me to continue freeing myself from the pain. As I began envisioning each treasured memory with *new* eyes, the sweet and bitter moments became wrapped in even deeper love and tucked away in my heart. Looking through this new lens of love, I realized I was free now to reclaim and experience our spiritual connections, knowing I was purifying my heart's pain.

During this process, I developed a valuable exercise as our memories unfolded before me. While finding another way to my memories after my loved one had passed, this exercise was an opportunity to open up to divine inspiration and heal. Only then was I able to experience the gratitude in having these moments show up on our path. Now I can say to myself: *I am now grateful for having these memories.*

The following phrases detail an intimate and personal recounting of some of my bitter and sweet memories. It is a picture of how my husband and I found moments of sharing our love and moments of relief from the challenges of living life through illness. You will see these underlined phrases that are <u>my own words,</u> revealing those precious moments. Further down, you will find phrases with blank spaces to fill in your own words.

I no longer <u>take in moments of pleasure etched on his face as he smiles,</u> *but I am now grateful for having this memory.*

I no longer <u>hug and rock him gently in bed while breathing whispers into his ear of sweet little songs,</u> *but I am now grateful for having this memory.*

I no longer experience sadness for his disappointment at being unable to express himself verbally, *but I am now grateful for having this memory.*

I no longer sense the laughter in his heart when I surprise him by saying something humorous, *but I am now grateful for having this memory.*

I no longer dash out to do errands, and return home with excitement in my heart and see he is *still there,* waiting for me, *but I am now grateful for having this memory.*

I no longer see his beautiful smile and the dimple on the left side of his face I so admired, *but I am now grateful for having this memory.*

I no longer feel the suffocating feeling in my heart when I realize his physicality will not be with me for long, *but I am now grateful for having this memory.*

I no longer find contentment in my heart when I glance over and see he is sleeping peacefully beside me, *but I am now grateful for having this memory.*

I no longer spend time creating new ways for him to navigate our home, *but I am now grateful for having this memory.*

I no longer enjoy reading to him at the bedside and when pausing, glancing up at his wide-eyed look of interest, *but I am now grateful for having this memory.*

I no longer find my breathing space nestled in his arms, *but I am now grateful for having this memory.*

I no longer <u>sense an inclination to get out of bed and tuck in the</u> <u>blankets around him to create a cozy barrier</u>, *but I am now grateful for having this memory.*

I no longer <u>carry around thoughts of his every need everywhere I go</u>, *but I am now grateful for having this memory.*

I no longer <u>sense his disappointment that physical limitations have</u> <u>changed him</u>, *but I am now grateful for having this memory.*

I no longer <u>feel tears in my eyes when he's not doing so well</u>, *but I am now grateful for having this memory.*

I no longer <u>find ways</u> <u>to keep his toes and fingers warm</u>, *but I am now grateful for having this memory.*

I no longer <u>revel in the look in his eyes when he suddenly realizes that</u> <u>I'm there to find my special place beside him</u>, *but I am now grateful for having this memory.*

I no longer <u>arrange for his special time to have a massage each week</u>, *but I am now grateful for having this memory.*

I no longer <u>wheel his chair to the window and view the colored leaves</u> <u>of fall, especially the red leaves on the maple tree</u>, *but I am now grateful for having this memory.*

I no longer <u>feel a sense of security while cuddling alongside him</u>, *but I am now grateful for having this memory.*

I no longer <u>smile with joy while watching him observe my every</u> <u>word</u>, *but I am now grateful for having this memory.*

I no longer <u>feel the morning urgency to rush to his bedside and greet</u> <u>him for the first time each new day</u>, *but I am now grateful for having this memory.*

I no longer <u>feel the pure harmony and warmth in our energy when I</u> <u>hug him</u>, *but I am now grateful for having this memory.*

I no longer <u>enjoy taking him to our favorite parks and embracing</u> <u>nature</u>, *but I am now grateful for having this memory.*

I no longer <u>sense my eyes brimming with love when he looks up at me</u> <u>and smiles with gratitude</u>, *but I am now grateful for having this memory.*

I no longer <u>linger with him outdoors at our home and enjoy the warm</u> <u>sunshine and cool breezes</u>, *but I am now grateful for having this memory.*

I no longer <u>take pleasure in showing him the flowers and small</u> <u>creatures scurrying around the walkways at our home</u>, *but I am now grateful for having this memory.*

I no longer <u>kneel at his bedside, caress his soft hand, and talk to him</u>, *but I am now grateful for having this memory.*

I no longer <u>neglect my rest to be with him, knowing this is *our* time</u> <u>now</u>, *but I am now grateful for having this memory.*

I no longer <u>feel helpless to take my eyes off him</u>, *but I am now grateful for having this memory.*

I no longer <u>admire his unrelenting courage and patience while</u> <u>dealing with his physical difficulties</u>, *but I am now grateful for having this memory.*

I no longer <u>feel happiness in my heart when our friends greet me</u> <u>with "How is Peter?" instead of "Hi, Tara,"</u> *but I am now grateful for having this memory.*

I no longer <u>feel hushed and healed by his kind words and sweet</u> <u>disposition,</u> *but I am now grateful for having this memory.*

I no longer <u>find my eyes darting around the shops and food stores</u> <u>while observing nearly everything has his name on it,</u> *but I am now grateful for having this memory.*

I no longer <u>slowly brush his hair as he closes his eyes and takes in</u> <u>feelings of pleasure,</u> *but I am now grateful for having this memory.*

I no longer <u>kiss his eyes softly while he is sleeping,</u> *but I am now grateful for having this memory.*

If you choose to try this exercise while experiencing the pain of your memories of a loved one, the following exercise and list of phrases with blank spaces is for you to write down your own words. You may want to reread your own words in the phrases many times until letting go of the pain is real to you.

While realizing that these losses can be turned into glorious gains, your new memories will strengthen you. As you look through a lens of love with new eyes and gratitude for having these experiences, the past becomes a beautiful source of joy.

EXERCISE:

1. While sitting in quietude, breathe deeply and relax.
2. Say the phrase, ***I no longer***, pause, and write down your own words.

3. While allowing these feelings to wash and wave through you, think of a gentle breeze on the ocean — let your emotions become peaceful.

4. Then finish the sentence by saying the phrase, ***but I am now grateful for having this memory.***

I no longer _____,
but I am now grateful for having this memory.

I no longer _____,
but I am now grateful for having this memory.

I no longer _____,
but I am now grateful for having this memory.

I no longer _____,
but I am now grateful for having this memory.

I no longer _____,
but I am now grateful for having this memory.

The glory of life consists of our ability to
feel deep and experience widely.

Chapter 20

Introduction to Channeled Transcriptions
(*After* Peter's Transition on November 2, 2013)

Five days after Peter made his transition from the physical realm to the spiritual realm; his higher self was available to give us a deep and subtle analysis of the breathtaking scope of his unique experience. His compelling words contain a small measure of the vast and astute knowledge of the collective consciousness that can only come from the pure experience of the higher self.

These next four chapters contain channeled transcriptions, recorded and transcribed verbatim, from the soul of Peter D. Conn. We offer these very personal and intimate recordings not only to share our journey in a personal way, but also for the opportunity to continue celebrating our legacy. Peter's inspiring words bring a new human face to spirituality, and they introduce another "life between lives" that Peter's soul and mine continue to share.

Perhaps it is time to open up to our loved ones on the other side. Our soul, the invisible part of us, has a yearning to be free — confined to the physical body makes the soul feel hemmed in.

There is a message in this for seekers who are willing to embrace our story about a deeper meaning of life after death. The death of the body makes way for the everlasting life of the soul, and passing is a glorious new existence in the spiritual world. It is not an ending.

In the continuum of life, we are eternal, for we never die or end. Communing with a loved one soul-to-soul in spirit is a profound event, and it can deepen our understanding of how giving spirit a voice can eliminate grief and benefit humanity.

NOTES: We suggest that the following channeled transcriptions, recorded and <u>transcribed verbatim,</u> are to be read in consecutive chapter order for continuity. All wording in boldface type is the voice of *the soul of Peter D. Conn.*

Appearing in italics, portions within the transcriptions indicate paraphrasing of comments/short conversations by the writer and channel/medium. These portions serve to inform the reader and are valuable for the continuity of subsequent paragraphs.

You never know where your soul will take you.

Chapter 21

Transcript of November 7, 2013
(Five Days after Peter's Transition)
Channeled by Laura Mirante, Channel/Medium

Tara: Peter, I am most grateful for this opportunity to commune with you in another divine state of awareness. These past five days have been marked not only by the the intense state of the grieving process, but by the joy of dedicating my heart and soul to the realities of the past and the emergence of our new journey. Our unbounded love stimulates my imagination to make our magnificent journey so far even more beautiful by feeling my sorrow with grace and noble acceptance. I am thrilled by this gift we have been blessed with representing the beginning of another grand journey. I love and honor your soul.

Laura: This will be our first channel with Peter from the great beyond since his passing five days ago on November 2, 2013. I'll just open up and see what Peter has to say.

The following channeled transcription was
recorded and transcribed verbatim:

Peter: I am free, dear one. I am in this moment available to you and also experiencing a divine reintegration of who I am. That's how I want to express what it is I am experiencing now. And I

153

know how often you think of where I am and what I could be doing, but I want to begin with the actual transition process. I want to give you my experience from this point of view, as you have already experienced it from that point of view, so you can begin to allow those two points of view to come together.

Let me begin by saying there was no trauma or stress there at the end. I simply slipped away. It was that simple, and it was that divine. I will say that it was an experience like none other; like *nothing* I experienced in the physical.

I often wondered what it would be like in that moment, in that instant where you leave the body. And it was just like that, just like I had expressed to you previously, that it was immediate recognition of something outside of myself giving me a sense of something more that I was a part of. It comes in as a wave of understanding, a wave of recognition, and then what occurs is a simple sense of knowing. There is almost a pull that comes from within that lifts you out of the physical and takes you into its arms and gently lays you in the energy of love and unconditional acceptance. That is what I perceived in the moment of transition. It was unconditional acceptance.

It's lighter than air, it's fluffier than the clouds, and it's much more comfortable than any comforter we can create on the earth plane. There is such a sense of airiness, of feather-lightness that you are. You do not feel any density. You do not feel any stagnation, any aches or pains or reminders of a physical body. You are simply energy; light as air in the midst of consciousness that is all around you. It is as if you are swimming in a sea of awareness and you are light as air. It is not even swimming, for swimming implies some kind of effort. You merely float. You think, you intend, and you move. It is as if I can just be in an instant anywhere I imagine. I can just imagine being with you, and then I am there. I can just imagine being in the energy of the trees of the Earth, and I am there. I can imagine being in the energy of the ocean, and in an instant I am there. It is that freeing, it is that fluid, and it is that self-serving that is the energy that takes you.

It allows you to know that any and all incarnations that you have are perfect, divine, and complete in themselves. There is no sense of anything or anyone missing. And although I do feel your devotion to me, I do not feel that I am missing you, for I *am* a part of your experience. And although we have not made that connection so definitively *in the physical*, I am still working through the kinks here, dear one. I haven't quite got it all figured out. I myself thought I would be much more fluid in communicating through these realms of existence that I am moving through, but I find it much more challenging than I thought. And although I speak as if intentionally I can be anywhere immediately, it is not that easy to manifest *in the physical*. I can be in the energy of the ocean, and the energy of the trees, and your energy, but, I have not perfected the art of manifesting *in the physical;* some kind of movement, some kind of significant signal for you to recognize as me. I'm still working on how it is I look to be in your experience in the physical.

I am working through the energies of the elementals, to show me how to move through the creatures of the earth plane. You know how some people like to believe that their loved ones exist in butterflies, birds, or other animals that come to visit? Well, I see now how that is possible ... how those gentle spirits allow us to move through them; how they give us a freedom to align with their energy so that we can get a glimpse of the physical world and give you a sense of our connectedness.

So, as the winter turns to spring, look for me in the creatures above the earth plane, for I know that I will be inhabiting many in different moments. There is no sense that I have to come into one and be that for the duration. I can see how fluid energy is and how interconnected we all are as souls. And yes, I will say quite clearly, that each of the individual creatures on the earth plane has a sense of a soul and has some spiritual aspect of who they are that defines the movements they have on the Earth. It is not that they are human inhabitants, and so their souls are of a different frequency, but they are still a part of the same energy that we are all connecting through. And so that is how you will recognize me in those moments where the animals seem to be trying to get your attention. Recognize it and give me some sense of acceptance, approval, and recognition of my efforts.

Let me bring you back to the idea that as I shifted, as I made my transition, I did find the love that Sally* was so much a part of and representing for me. It was as if she took up that role for me and allowed me to find her. It was not so much that I had to find the religious image I thought I would be meeting. It was quite interesting to see dear old Sally* there in the light, saying, *yes, this is exactly how you do it, and this is exactly where you belong.* She was more than willing to be that for me, as I know she is for many. And although I did find myself surrounded by many of the familiars, I did not recognize them with the same intensity that I did dear Sally*. And I see now how making these kinds of connections on the earth plane is supported in our spiritual experience.

Let me tell you, there was another gift here for me. There was a loved one that I had been missing for quite some time that I was able to embrace in an energy of truth that allowed me to see our experience together in a new light. I would say that he was one, in my experience, that had a major influence on who I was to be. And although I only had him in my life for a short while, I recognize now the kind of influence people can have on you, even if they are only in your experience for a short while. So I want you to know that I did find my friend, and I did recognize the kind of connection we had was much more than what it appeared to be in the physical. I can only say to you now, that it was your willingness to be open to that energy that allowed me to make that connection so immediately. And I thank you for that. It is not one that you could possibly understand in the physical. It's much more ethereal than I can even define for you. So I will not even try. I will leave it at that and let you know that what happens when you transition is a coming together of souls that love you, a coming together of souls that are here to support you.

And yes, my dear, even your soul, your soul was here in the light. You may not consciously comprehend what it is I am expressing to you, but it is that higher aspect of self that exists beyond the physical that was here for me, that embraced me just as I embrace you now.

We are more, so much more than just our physical bodies. There are aspects of ourselves that exist beyond the physical experience, and there are many, many levels to our truth. That is something I am coming to terms with now, in this moment, that truth is not so simple. It is not so cut-and-dried and black-and-white, and it is not something that can be defined according to the rights and wrongs of the world.

As you move through this transition process, you begin to see how far off we were as the human beings that we were. And I do not mean me personally as an individual that I was far from my soul's purpose. I am not saying that at all. I aligned quite nicely with my highest purpose, and I did my best to honor my soul in the ways that I could with the limitations I had as the human being that I was. But what I am saying is, as a community. As a community, we have gone so far from our truth. We have created a society that supports this distance that we have created. And it is going to be some treacherous journey for many of the young ones coming into this world, in this time, to try to redirect the flow of energy in this society. And although there is much to be grateful for and much to be appreciative of, there is much in this experience that really does stretch our ability to perceive who we truly are.

It is a grand and glorious effort that we make when we come there in the physical and try to surpass the fearful inclinations of the logical mind and the body and the ego. It is quite a challenge to the soul to see how far our mind can take us from our truth. And it is really quite something to come back together, come back into our truth wholeheartedly, embracing our divinity. That's what happens, you know, at the instant you let go of the physical, you fully embrace the idea that you are divine.

Oh, I cannot speak for everyone. I will just say that's how it was for me, that I could not let myself be in that physical body any longer. It just felt so restrictive. It felt so limited and so filled with uncertainty. And so I see the profound awareness that comes with the letting go of the body, mind, and ego. It's as if you are flooded with awareness, with the wisdom of generations of experience. And it does take you. It takes you away, it takes you far from the physical world interpretation of who you thought you were. And it does allow you to recognize how profound each and every experience in your life has been and how often you did not give yourself full permission to experience it all.

I see that I did that. I did limit my ability to experience life more from the soul's point of view, well, at least up until the end. Then I was all about the soul, wasn't I? It was all about the soulful experience, and I see how I needed that ... and how much it helped me to make this transition. For if I had not had that experience, I would not have made such a soulful connection with you and with myself, and with so many others. I never would have set out to make that effort. And so I see how the soul did allow me to use that experience to create a more complete connection. It is as if I closed the circuit, and the energy was able to flow in its authentic nature, in its totality. And that's all you can really ask for in a transition is to be fully aware of what it is you are experiencing.

I see now that there are others that are not aware of what they are going through, the ones that deny that it's their potential future. They exist in the illness in hopes that it will not end in this way. And that is simply an untruth that they tell themselves, for each and every individual moving through this process has some awareness of it. And the more connected they are with their soul and their higher self, the more that awareness can show through.

Then we are given the option as the human beings that we are to make that choice: to embrace the idea that transition is a beautiful part of the human experience, or, to fight the unknown. And as they chose to fight the unknown, they created that block in them to this kind of open transitional process. And although there is something to be experienced other than the perfect, smooth transition, it is one that I recommend taking.

It really does make a difference, you know, how open you are to the idea of dying or to the idea that you do not die at all. It really does help to know that there is no death. It takes the fear out of the process. I can't say that I know too much more than I did when I was there, although it does appear to be flowing through me quite nicely in this moment. And as I speak with you, dear one, I want you to know that I myself am as amazed at my awareness as you are.

I am beginning to come to terms with the idea that I was there for so long without ever really engaging you. I did not experience the time while I was in my disconnect. So for me, it was only a day or two; not fully recognizing how many of those days went by, and how often you came to sit with me, to be with me, to bring me your beautiful energy. I see that now much more clearly. It was a bit of a haze there for me, as I was in between worlds. And now that I can see more clearly, I see how dedicated you were and are, and how devoted to my experience you became. And I thank you for that. I will be eternally grateful for the way you gave so much of your experience over to mine. I must give you that sense of appreciation, for I want you to know there was nothing more you could do for me than what you did. And you did so much more than I ever would have expected you to. I want you to know that. I want you to know how grateful I am for allowing me to have the experience I did.

Many would have given up hope long ago and would have possibly put me in some institution that could have better cared for me physically, but not you, my dear; you found a way. You found a way for us to be together through the entire experience, and for that, I will be forever grateful, and I will forever be at *your* side.

I do realize now that you do not recognize me, but you will. You will, my dear. As the grief begins to subside, you will begin to find moments of connectedness and moments of lightness where you will know and recognize my energy. In this moment when I begin to surface in your awareness, the grief begins to come, and that is a natural process. For what you are doing is connecting the idea of me with the idea that I am no longer there. And that is a tragic part of the human perception of life, you know. It is something that we look to shift as a generation so that in the future, we do not have to have that sense of disconnect. I want to say, have that initial sense of disconnect, for that is how I see it. I know it will not last. I know our connection is too strong for this separation to remain.

So just realize that as I work through my process, and you work through your process, we will come back together in the exact moment that we are ready for what we will be experiencing together. The subtle movements are already in motion. I am working to rearrange some of the things in the home to give you a sense that I can. And, so, as I begin to do this, do not get angry that I have shifted things around, but rather realize that it is a big production for me to try and make something in the physical move.

I am in awe of how dense our physicality is and how airy our energy is, and how they have to come together at some point to make this life work. I am in awe that it works; that's what I will say. I am in awe of the human experience because it seems impossible from this point of view, from this aspect of who I am, to believe I could become that dense. It is just like you trying to perceive yourself as a spirit, as a soul, as light and airy. It's difficult because you are in a body that is so dense, so configured in the physical that you can't find the attachments to spirit.

Take your time, dear one; take each step one at a time. Do not feel that you have to rush through any of this process. Realize that it is an integration for you of a new way of being. That is what you are experiencing. It is not so much about a loss, my dear, but about a gain, a gain of a new way of experiencing life. That is what you are moving through. And don't ever dismiss that you, yourself are moving through a transitional process. I want you to honor that. I want you to recognize that in the future, you will be changed. You will be a different you because of this transitional process, just as I am a different me.

There is so much I want to share with you. And I want to say that your relatives are here as well. I am with your maternal grandmother more than I am with mine, and I find that quite interesting. I see that we have such a strong connection that I cannot explain to you how deeply I feel for her.

Laura: Tara, did you want to say something about that?

Tara: Well… I… that I never met her. She had died before I was born, and I was very … please give me a minute here.

Laura: You know her name?

Tara: I was very young. She died at forty-seven … she had a heart attack … or stroke.

Laura: What was her name? What was her name?

Tara: I hear you, but I don't know for sure … I can't seem to remember — I feel so confused at this point … I'm astounded to learn that Peter ...

Laura: Okay, that's okay, you don't have to; he knows who it is.

Tara: At this moment, I'm overwhelmed to hear that Peter is with my maternal grandmother … and I … I never met her.

Laura: All right, let me let him keep going.

Peter: I can only say that she has experienced our life with us and that you and she have a bond like soul mates in the energy. It is really quite interesting to think that you did not even experience her in life, and yet she is so prominent in my transition. It does make you question all that we think we know about our connections in the physical, doesn't it? It helps you to stretch to the idea that our connections are much more energetic than they are familial. I like to give you that kind of awareness so that you can ponder the bigger aspects of who we are as individuals. It is wonderful to see how you engage these kinds of experiences and allow the energy of these communications to work within your awareness, to shift your perception of life.

And, so, I will continue to give you a sense of what I am experiencing here. There were more energies than just that of the maternal grandmother and Sally*. I must say, that it is an army of supporters that come; some of them you recognize from this life, and some of them you recognize from previous experiences. Not that they are defined intellectually for you in the moment; it is just the awareness of the recognition, the awareness of the familiarity that comes. You immediately feel embraced by old friends and by wise teachers. It's an interesting combination, but that's how it comes forth, at least for me. It appears as if they line up to give you a sense of their effect on your life in an instant. In an instant, you are aware completely of how they were a part of your experience. And yet in this instant, I couldn't tell you, I couldn't tell you in one sentence where each of them fits in my life. I could not think of the exact experiences, but the awareness comes to me in the knowingness.

Many aspects ... ah, many aspects of the human condition seem to surface as you rise above the human condition. It is as if you feel all of the lower-frequency energies trying to hold on, trying to give you something to hold onto in the physical, in case you're not ready — in case you are looking to continue the experience. And yet there is an awareness, there is a certainty that this is the time and that 'all that' is what you are leaving behind, and it almost spurs you into a state of gratitude, immediately.

For when you feel all the negativity of the human experience, and you feel the freedom of letting go of it, you find yourself in an expanse defined only by the endlessness of love. I cannot seem to find the words to fully embrace what I am trying to convey here. Love just doesn't do it. I know we have a certain experience of what love is, but it is nothing … it is nothing compared to what I am experiencing. I am in an ocean of unconditional acceptance, and even that idea and that image isn't quite enough to give you a sense of what it is I am experiencing. Fluidity is a word that I choose, for that is what I feel now; fluid, moving in motion, in constant motion. And isn't that a change for me from what I was just experiencing in the physical? It's quite something, for what I see is how fluid I was in spirit while my body was so stagnant.

And I see that that is … ah, that it is that way for most human beings which is why the greats, like Jesus and Buddha, took their leave, took their moments of detachment from the physical experience to find their truth. You will find in many of the stories of the great ones that it was those opportunities they gave themselves to detach completely from the physical world that allowed them to reconnect with their truth. It's as if they themselves created their own transitional process while remaining in the physical, and that truly is something to be honored. And although I see religion now from a much different point of view, I do feel that honoring each and every one of those brilliant aspects of truth is worthy.

But I do not feel that any of them wanted their legacy to be what it has become. And that's a restriction in the physical world that is going to shift. That is going to change where life does not have to limit what it is a human being has created by the interpretations of others, but rather, that it will allow spirit to continue the energy of that human intention without the limitations of others' perceptions. So, when you see the image of the Buddha, you can honor that Buddha in the same way you honor the Christ; and you can know that Mohammad had the same pure intentions for sharing the truth that many others did, such as the ancients of the Eastern Worlds. Lao-tzu and Confucius both held quite an enormous energy of integrity and looked only to share the truth.

And so we can see that there is no one individual that has come with the quote-unquote, right truth, but rather that their lives are examples of how to find your own truth. And, what we lost in the creation of our religions is the idea that our own truth is individual and unique; and that we each must find our own way to our own truth, not that we must follow along with someone else's truth. They all taught that, you know. The body, mind, and ego may not have interpreted it quite so freely, but it's there in their teachings — the idea that their way is not to be mimicked, but rather to be learned from.

Tara: Thank you Peter. Thank you for your astute and incisive grasp of these insights.

Tara talks about writing and asks Peter to comment on her writing a book about their journey.

Peter: Share, share, and share again; share with anyone that will listen. This is most certainly the most impactful information that human beings need to assimilate now. And if they can hear it, and if they can be willing enough to believe it, they can shift their own experience. And you know that just from your experience. You know that several years ago, you would have experienced this transition in a much more unenlightened way.

I'm so excited, my dear, for I feel that this is our next journey together. To be able to do this and share this and allow other people to benefit from it — well, why else would we have this kind of experience if not to help others? Doesn't that just make sense? Doesn't it just seem to be the natural flow of events? And as you have already seen, it *is* a natural flow, isn't it? As I said in a previous channel, I know that you will know who to speak with, who to share with. They will come to you.

That's the way it works in the energy. As your willingness extends in the field, their openness responds, and then your energies are brought together. That is the way life experience seems to work; where there is a willingness to give and an openness to receive, those energies come together. And so I want you to recognize that it will not be that you'll have to try to figure it out; you will not have to make a plan and find a way. It will be as if it falls into place.

Every little bit and piece of this puzzle will appear before you exactly when you need it. Just trust that idea and know that we will do this together. I have much to share and much to offer as far as the information I am beginning to assimilate. And as I do, I want to continue to communicate it to you so that you can share it with others. There is a sense of importance in this that I know that you feel, and I want you to honor that.

So, as you step out of the mundane that you have been existing in and begin to extend yourself in many different directions, you will feel the tap on the shoulder, here and there when it is your time to share. And as far as writing it … yes my dear, it will write itself, and it is something worth the effort. Singing is not the only way you can use your voice, you know, although it is quite eloquent. You do have a way with words yourself, and you have a way of instigating intrigue in others. You're quite the storyteller, my dear, and when you begin to convey this story, you will find that the energy itself will attract many to hear it. And so I say, let's do this, let's do this together and let's show people how it's done.

It's not just about channeling with the higher self with someone who is incapable of communicating in the physical, and it's not just about channeling with a loved one on the other side. Oh no, my dear, it is much more grand, much more expansive than this. What you are talking about is communing through life soul-to-soul, regardless of whether the soul is in the physical or in the spiritual. That's what we want to begin to understand and appreciate and live from; that idea that we are souls here having a physical experience, and it does not matter whether we have a body or not.

You see, I am here in a physical experience with you, my energy is. I may not have a physical body in this moment to maneuver the earth plane, so all I have to work with is your hope and your connection to me. So you can see how important it is to those in spirit to find people to be open to this kind of communication. For when we extend ourselves in that direction and are not received, we are not able to inject ourselves so openly in your experience. It is a back and forth here in this kind of experience.

There is a commitment that must be made between souls where the human being values the efforts that the soul is making to be a part of the experience. And, just in recognizing it, the human being extends himself just in valuing a sign here or there. The human being extends his energy into the spiritual realm just by intention. And, that is so much of what you want to share, that what we have learned through this experience is that it does not matter what the body, the mind, or the ego is doing, the soul lives.

Tara explains that she hopes to take our story to a well-known self-help author and spiritual awareness teacher to acquire his support for our efforts to bring our story through and into the world.

Peter: You may want to consider allowing him to experience more of our journey together while I was there. It's much more impressive and much more awakening than this kind of information. And although I do have a unique interpretation of what it is like here on the other side, there are others in the physical that already create those kinds of images in human consciousness. And so, the idea that you have that takes this spiritual awareness to the next level is the idea that we communed soulfully while my body was not quite functioning the way that it is expected to. That in itself is an enormous shift in the way people will view our ability to commune soul-to-soul.

Our experience is much more grand than even that is if you consider how we configured the movements of the souls, I mean, the movements of the human beings through our soul awareness to have the kind of experience that we have, and to make the kind of connections that we made in order to have this experience. You can see how far back that beginning point really is. It goes back to our conception, dear one, when we came into this world, already knowing that this is the kind of experience we were coming into.

Tara: I treasure our magnificent journey and how it turned out in the end.

Peter: It is not the end. It is not the end at all, my dear; it is just the beginning of a new phase of our experience together. Do not ever dismiss that idea that we are still in this together. You must recognize that our soulful connection is stronger than any sense of separation we may perceive. It is in your heart that I will always remind you I exist, and it is in there that you will find me. In your moments of uncertainty, focus all of your attention there, and know that that is where I live; that is where I exist. There is no other place for me to be. That is where I belong, and that is where I will remain.

And I will inspire you from there. I will attract the kinds of experiences that will have us both knowing we are so much more powerful than we ever knew. That is our journey together, and it is not at all close to being over. So, just recognize that we are in this for the long haul and that there is much for us to do together, and we can affect many because of our experience together. There is so much more that I will be engaging that I will want to share with you. And as I do, you will then share with others. There's going to be a magnificent ripple effect in the consciousness of the human experience. Do not ever dismiss the power that we have to affect others. There is truly a purpose for this experience, and we are not going to let that go.

Tara: Thank you, my love. I am so excited and so pleased to receive your full reassurance that our grand journey together will continue to support others in search of soulful awareness. I cherish the unfoldment of our experiences now and in the future.

Peter, I am interested in knowing if many will be open to this kind of spiritual connection.

Peter: You'd be surprised how many more people are open than we ever thought. It is a movement that I see growing on the earth plane. And I believe that that is why we are here in this time because there is the availability of receptivity; where there is enough openness for this information to be integrated in a consciously aware state of acceptance. You see, if the information comes in and nobody buys it, nobody believes it, nobody integrates it into their logical mind, well, it kind of just bounces off the collective consciousness. But, the fact that there are many, many thousands, even millions, that are now aware of our spiritual connection, well, it does open up to taking our understanding of our soulful connection to a new level. The openness is already there, my dear; we just need to bring forth the new information and allow them to integrate it as well.

Tara: Peter, while tasting the joys and sorrows of my grieving process, I intend to continue transcribing all of our recorded channeled sessions through the time that I will be writing about our grand journey.

Peter: I believe it will be a very healing process for you to take this initiative and to transcribe these words, for what I see is that these words are filled with astute energy. And as you do it, that energy becomes a part of who you are. That awareness is immediately integrated into your field, which will bring you such a sense of peace and a sense of knowing in the continuity of life. That is so important for you in this moment. And so I say to you, my dear, that you are already reflecting my truth in your experience. Realize that these inspirations, these desires and inclinations that you are feeling, they do not come strictly from your logical mind,

but, rather they're coming from the inspirations that I and others here are conveying to you energetically.

You want to recognize that that is one way that I will be able to commune with you. I will drop bits and pieces of information in your mind, little insights that inspire you in one direction or another. And that is where you want to be confident in those moments. When you receive those bits and pieces of insights, you want to move confidently forward in that direction, knowing that you are honoring a soulful intuitive understanding of how the energy works in this world.

I am so pleased that you are willing to engage me in this way, and I am so pleased that you are extending yourself in the world through the creative arts. And remember my words, dear one: you have many more creative talents than you have allowed yourself to recognize. So continue to explore new ways to express your creativity, and know that I am behind each and every new experience that you have. I want you to continue to experience the newness of life, for that is how I can experience it as well with you. And know that I am with you always and that I will remain here in this energy of truth for you to tap into any time that you feel. We will continue to strengthen our intuitive connection to one another, but don't worry about that now. Just move through this process, and allow the healing energies to take you over and inspire in you a sense of direction. It will come, my dear; you will know in a moment which direction to move in and what step to take. Just be confident in your intuitive sense of knowing and follow my direction.

I am in your heart and in your soul always. We are one energy, dear one; we are one energy that moves fluidly through this experience together. I will remain with you throughout your

days here, and I will be here to greet you when it is your time. But do not make that time come any sooner than it is astute for you soulfully, for I will be here for you regardless.

Tara: Peter, I am enormously grateful for *all* of the beautiful gifts you continue to bring to me. You have no idea how moved I am by our conversations. I am amused by the emotions felt by remembering your unique personality and smile that you displayed so well when I knew you on the earth plane, as Peter. I adore you, and I honor you.

[End of session/ tape.]

"To die is different from what anyone supposed, and luckier."
— Walt Whitman

Chapter 22

Transcript of January 24, 2014
(Twelve Weeks after Peter's Transition)
Channeled by Laura Mirante, Channel/Medium

Tara expresses her love for Peter and her continued gratitude and amazement at their ability to reach each other on this interdimensional level.

Tara informs Peter that she has had the wonderful pleasure of communicating with his granddaughter, Kelly.

Tara offers the platform to Peter.

> *The following channeled transcription was recorded and transcribed verbatim:*

Peter: I am at a juncture in my transition that is asking of me to fulfill certain commitments that I had prior to incarnation, and reconnecting with this young one [his granddaughter, Kelly] **is a part of what it is I set out to do. And so I would say, thank you for reaching out to her and continuing my legacy, for she is a part of my history. She is a part of my energy and she is a part of my bloodline. And so there is a lot of *me* in *her,* and that is something you may see, my dear. You may see certain inclinations**

and certain idiosyncrasies that I had that she may have somehow picked up on. It's as if it moved through our lineage and not through any kind of imprinting. I see that so much of who we become is determined more by our energy than by our actual human family. It's more about what we hand down energetically than what we take on in the physical. It's all already determined prior to incarnation, and I am seeing it much more clearly now than I could have if I were there.

That's something I wish to tell you about — that there is a sense of clarity now, such a sense of clarity. Although I may have appeared to you as being clear in our communications, it was not quite so for me in my interpretation of what it was I was experiencing. The cloudiness or the haze actually did affect my ability to integrate *all* that I was experiencing. So it was wonderful of you to mark it energetically, and that is what you did each and every time that you engaged this kind of communication. You allowed my experience to be recorded, energetically. You allowed what I was feeling and experiencing in the moment to be recorded.

And you did so with an authentic nature that was not defined by any human desire or intent, and that is the beauty of it, my dear. It was always about just letting me speak, just letting me be a part of the experience, just allowing me to be recognized as whole and complete when everybody else around would look at me and feel as though I was missing a part of me, a big part of me. And I would say it really wasn't so. I really didn't feel like I was missing much at all, but rather that I was having a much deeper, a much more profound experience than most of the human beings. And I know that you felt it as well, that we were able to have that experience together.

And I will say, from my perspective, not many can do it; not many can do what you did for me. I want you to know that. And I want you to hear it quite clearly that you do not give yourself enough credit for all that you have been through, and all that you are going through, and all that you did and do for me on a continual basis. You have to give yourself credit, dear one. You really do stand above the crowd here in this kind of a situation, with this kind of a human perception of what is occurring. For you to be able to rise above the normal interpretation of what I was experiencing and go with me as far as you did ... it is absolutely incredible, and something to be marked as divine and unique in you. You tend to give me all the credit, my dear, and I wish that you wouldn't. I wish that you would hold yourself on a much higher platform, so that you can see how beautiful, how strong and intent you are.

I am certainly amazed at how easy it is [laughter] for me to come through you. It is quite something, isn't it, dear one, to be able to know that we are merging on a conscious level? That somewhere out there in the ethers, our energies are communing, are dancing if you will, and then we create together what you are writing there in your world. I want you to know that it's not just me telling you what to write; it's you and I, dear one, it is you and I together.

We are here in the energy and dancing like young ones and enjoying our true youthfulness, for that is what I feel here in spirit; as if I were twenty again, as if we had just met and were in our healthiest stage of life. That is what it feels like, and you are here with me. It's something for you to consider now, being there on the earth plane, the idea that I have a piece of you. Yes, in my heart, if you wish to view it that way, but it's with me, and it stays with me, and it will always stay with me. And we, in this state of being, continually dance together, and as we do, we create together.

And that is what inspires you to write — our joining, dear one, our communing together as souls. It is not just Peter telling you what to do; you must dismiss this thought. I do not want you to look at me as being your puppeteer. I will not accept that as the definition of you, and you cannot either. You must see this as a joint effort, where the two of us are doing this together, and there is no way either of us could do it without the other. Can you fully appreciate the intensity of that statement from me? I just wanted to make that clear, for I feel that in your moments of uncertainty, you really do dismiss your true power and potential and I don't want to see that from you, my dear. You are too powerful, too beautiful, and you exist from a state of mind that is influenced only by the energy of integrity. We are a team, my dear, and we will remain that way. This is not about me alone; this is about our journey together. Please remember that. Please remember that you are the most important part of my journey, and so how can I have a journey if it is not ours?

Tara: Peter, my heart is overcome by your beautiful thoughts and energy. I thank you, my love, I thank *you* for being here for *me*.

Tara comments on the inspirations she receives while writing; it's as if Peter's words are moving through her.

Peter: That is the way you would view it as the human being that you are, and when you are in spirit, you are able to expand your understanding of what life is all about. And so that is what I am doing here in this moment, allowing you to recognize the depth of the connection we have, that it is not about me, the individual human being anymore. Our souls are combined, my love; our souls are one. And when I inspire you in a certain direction, believe me, my dear, that energy takes on a color or a flair that can only come from you. So as those words get put down on paper, they are a combination of my intent and your intelligence. Do not dismiss that. You are as much a part of each and every word as I am. And I want you to accept that as a truth. I want you to know that there is nothing there that is only me coming through you; that as I inspire you, you take that inspirational energy, and then you add yours to it. And that, my dear, is how we create together.

It is a time in history that is saying it's time to appreciate the soulful connection we have to our loved ones in spirit. That is where we are as a collective, you know. We're at that juncture in the human history where it is time to let go of the fear of the unknown, of the fear of death, and the fear and uncertainty of what exists beyond this physical world that we can't see with our physical eyes.

It's people like you and [me], my dear, that are going to break down so many of those limiting belief systems. We are going to advance the human potential to integrate the higher awareness available to all with the willingness to open up to loved ones from the other side. Why should we be the lucky ones? Why should we be the only ones having these kinds of exchanges? There is so much more for the human being to experience through this kind of interacting. It is time for others to recognize that it is not only possible, but it is a necessary part of the human evolution. And that although we did look to separate, detach, and create the illusion of individuality to have this human experience, we have evolved to a point where we are capable of beginning to integrate this higher awareness that knows that we are all having this experience together ... that we never actually leave the experience; that we never actually die or end.

Tara: Peter, is it more difficult for a man in our society to find his way, soulfully?

Peter: There is such a deep desire in a man to take this seeker's journey, but then you know how it goes. You understand the body, mind, and ego. And it's almost as if a man in this culture must have some drastic experience to provide him the freedom to feel entitled to do this soulful seeking, such as I have. I had to have that major experience before I would allow myself to go this far with this soulful understanding.

Again, you can see how difficult we make it for ourselves as human beings. It's just that when a man gets a sense of it, he has to take that sense into his logical mind and define it intellectually, and then everything shifts, doesn't it? So many people go through this all alone. They don't realize that there is a support system out there, that there are others out there that can acknowledge your truth and support you in it. Because of his unwillingness to be this for others in his life, he feels he cannot ask this of others.

It is time, and it is through mediums and channels like Laura and Sally* that the world is being blessed with this kind of understanding. There are many others out there now doing this kind of work and expanding the human's ability to entertain these high-frequency notions. So, as you step into this kind of arena and you take on this kind of responsibility — and that is what you are doing, my dear — it is a tremendous responsibility that you have taken on, this idea that you are willing to share this

journey and your experiences and our experiences, and you are willing to stand up for a truth that you not only believe exists but that you know you have experienced.

I want to say that this is the easy part. This is the part where you are just creating the foundation to move forward, and it is flowing quite nicely, I would say. I would continue to look for more signs, more signals, if you will, of the direction with which you will take this endeavor. It will come to you exactly at the moments that you need to know. You will be given those kinds of signs and signals, and you will know within your heart what it is I am conveying to you. I only redirect the creative energy that you extend in this world. That is how I see it. Your soul is dictating the movements here. I only support you by giving you the signs, the definitive signals in the physical world that allow you to know that you are not doing this alone, rather that we are doing this together. And when I say *we,* I don't mean just me up here and you down there. I mean you up here as well. And I say *up here* just to reference the higher aspect of you engaging this experience. I must continue to remind you that there is a part of you here in spirit with me that is working through you to create the opportunities for this manifestation of truth.

Tara: Peter, how do you think those who know you will receive our book?

Peter: Ah, yes … the book will be an eye-opening experience for many that knew me and many that didn't. It will certainly bring to light our truth and give people much to ponder.

Tara: Peter, can you please comment on those who are not interested in sharing our experience? Thank you.

Peter: I would not feel that it is your responsibility, dear one; that's how I want to say it. I want you to let that go. You do not

have to worry or be concerned about how people receive you. It's important for you to hear that right now, up front before you really put yourself out there. I want you to recognize that it is not up to you what people do with the information we share. Our job is to share it and let it go. Let it be what it is to each and every person that receives it. They're going to receive it in their own way, and they're going to benefit from it in their own way. That's what you want to remember, that the soul's journey is a unique journey. And so we cannot compare, we cannot judge, and we cannot think we know what each soul needs. So, when you look at that human being and you think, *well, their life would be so much better off if they had this understanding,* you cannot possibly expect to understand what it is that soul came to experience.

Although the human being may benefit from this kind of awareness, if it is not aligned with a soulful purpose, it will not be heard. That is simply the truth of our existence. If we are not meant to be in that energy for our growth, we will not be in it; even if it is placed right in our lap, we will not acknowledge it. We will not see it, and we will not integrate it. So don't worry about it. The people who need to benefit from it will, and those that can't hear it — you will know that they are on a different journey. And that is how you will accept it and let them go.

You do not want to attach anything to anybody else's interpretation of your experience. You do not want to define who you are, your ability to be authentic and true, and you do not want to defend your truth. You simply want to share your perspective of the situation and let people do what they will with the information you share. You are not here to change anybody's mind or insist anybody believe what you believe. You just know that you believe what you believe because you know what you know because you've experienced what you've experienced, and you let that be enough. And you let that be all that you need, and you let everything else go.

Tara talks to Peter about plans for the book and the synchronistic connections she is making in conversations with a staff member at the Alzheimer's-Parkinson's Association (where she called about donating Peter's medical equipment). She was asked if she would speak at one of their caregiver meetings once our book is available.

Tara: Peter, I am inspired to request our local newspaper to repost some of your *Prose and Conn* commentaries written in 1967, as a "time capsule," and in your memory.

Peter: I think it is wonderful, my dear, that you are able to see the continuity and the flow of life through your experiences and through the interactions you are having. I do believe that if they are willing to repost those — I don't want to say the editorials, but the *Prose and Conn* — that it will inspire others, and it will bring a little bit of me back into that energy. And I think that's always a good thing.

I am amazed at how open you are to following these leads if you will, these spiritual directives. That is what is occurring now. This Association is a perfect platform; it is the exact platform that we want to address. These are the people that we want to reach, that we want to touch, that we want to give some hope and inspiration. So, of course, they would be the ones calling on you, for that is the way you set it up, my dear. You set it up so that it wouldn't be difficult for you, so that you would understand that each and every step would show up exactly when you needed it to. And that's what's happening, and that is what you are seeing.

And isn't it a magnificent way to appreciate the interconnected nature of the life experience. This is a magnificent time for both of us, for me to see how graciously and gracefully you move through this physical world with the steps that are illuminated through the faith that you carry. That is what does it, you know. That is why those who have little faith cannot find their way in this world. The faith truly does light the way. And that is why our connection is so strong, because you, my dear, because you are able to keep that faith, because you are able to keep me alive through your willingness to be open to my life-force energy. That's the way I see it.

As far as the coincidences occurring in your life, I think you will find that the more you recognize the connected nature of them, the more they will occur. I think you will feel in time that life is simply surreal; that there is no level of practicality that will sustain you the way the inspirations seem to guide you. That is how you are going to let go of the practical side of you that is looking to follow some linear plan.

You're going to see that these random, spontaneous synchronicities are truly the directives of the soul and that you do not need that logical plan; that the *soul* is already showing you the plan. And the soul is not going to show you that end result. It's not going to let you know exactly what the goal is. Right now, you believe you have a goal, but our goal is much more expansive than anything you have even considered yet. So just continue to be open, and continue to allow your soul to give you a sense of our connected intention to bring peace into the hearts of those that are experiencing life with a loved one that experiences the situation I did.

I want to leave you with this intense desire I have to continue to remind you that we are doing this together. I cannot say it enough. I cannot convey to you how important it is for you to see yourself as powerful as you see me. We must give ourselves that kind of respect where you respect yourself as much as you respect me. I cannot, in good conscience, continue forward if I believe that you are going to keep me on some pedestal above you. I must be on an equal playing field as you. You must feel as powerful as I for us to accomplish what it is we are setting out to do. I want you to recognize that that is how we are able to commune when we see each other as equals, when we respect each other's individuality and connectedness. It is that, that keeps us going. It is that, that keeps us connected and keeps that line of communication open. I will always be here in the energy of you, so continue to find me there and know that we are one.

Tara: Peter, thank you, for your wonderful words of wisdom. I am very grateful.

What do you think about this as a proposed title for our book: *Our Grand Journey of Self-Exploration?*

Peter: As a title, it certainly does encompass exactly what it is we are setting out to share. I feel that it may expand over time, but that it's a beautiful place to start.

Tara tells Peter of her interesting experience, reading the volumes of news clips about his career in state government when he was in his late twenties and into his thirties.

Peter: I don't want you to get lost in it all. It was just another way for you and I to get even closer, for the more you know me, the more we open up to each other energetically.

Tara: Thank you, Peter. This has truly been an extraordinary experience. I love you dearly, I honor you, and I will always be a part of you.

[End of session/tape.]

Chapter 23

Transcript of April 10, 2014

(Approximately Five Months after Peter's Transition)
Channeled by Laura Mirante, Channel/Medium

Tara: Peter, I am in limitless gratitude for this opportunity to commune with you, and I marvel at your ability to reach me. I think of you all the time, and I miss you very much.

Peter, will you again please speak to the issue of how someone in your similar situation (before the transition), will be receptive to our message?

Tara gives Peter the platform.

> *The following channeled transcription was*
> *recorded and transcribed verbatim:*

Peter: I cannot emphasize enough how accepting you are, how open you are, and how receptive you are to my energy. I want you to know that this is our truth, that this is truly what we came here to experience together. And it may baffle some logical minds to think that this is what we came to do, that this was our greatest purpose, and that this will be our legacy, but it is true. It is what we are accomplishing together now that will shake the foundation of many people's lives, that will allow them to begin

to expand beyond the limiting interpretation of what someone in my situation is experiencing.

As we begin to open the minds of others that are in this similar situation [as I was], you will begin to feel resistance, my dear, and I want to bring that to the forefront of your awareness. I want to proactively engage you in this way so that you are prepared; so that you realize that this world is filled with many different types of people, having many different types of experiences, coming from many different levels of consciousness. And so some will embrace you, and some will honor you for your willingness to put our experience out there like this. Then again, some may just refute the information as ridiculous and illogical. And when this occurs, my dear, you will find in you a sense of insecurity surfacing. Although you are so certain of what we've experienced together, there will come that point where the logical mind will say: *How can I be so far from what other people, other human beings, believe in this world?* And you know that that is what this is. It's so far from what other people are willing to believe. It takes them to a place in their interpretation of life that they are afraid to re-explore, you see.

When someone is so certain about the idea that this illness, this affliction is so debilitating for the soul experiencing it, they cannot fathom the idea that the soul is actually flourishing through and *because* of that experience. It is a difficult thing for a human being to do, to take themselves out of their personal conviction that they are victim to this experience and that the one they love that is going through it is a victim to it as well. They have a difficult time believing that the soul could actually bring the human being this experience for some opportunity for growth because, in the logical mind, growth shows some intellectual advancement. And what can be defined as intellectual advancement in human form is not what we've experienced together.

I want to say that we've both expanded because of this situation. We've both grown and developed our own state of awareness of the limitless nature of our human expression. This is the part of us that exists beyond the human being but integrates the human experience into the collective awareness of what it is to be an energy in a physical body.

So you, my dear, through your willingness, have created for us this opportunity to expand together in our own subconscious, the conscious understanding of our soulful connection, and the way we can use that connection to bring about change in our world. It was never just about us figuring it out and then allowing ourselves to benefit from it. You know as well as I do that both of us have always felt that what we benefit from, we want to share in this world. We want to give to others so that they can then feel as we feel, so blessed and so honored to be so gifted through our experience in this world.

I must say that you are appreciating our interactions now in a way I never could have if it was me there on the Earth. And I must continue to reiterate that we are each exactly where we need to be. For I could not have done what it is you've done for me, as I could not have imagined this experience from your point of view. I could not have seen me taking those same steps, reacting in the same ways, or allowing with grace and dignity as you have. So you must continue to remind yourself that this is a two-sided adventure; you are bringing the physical side, and I am bringing the spiritual side, and we're bringing it together.

That is a reflection of the big picture occurring now. That is what is going on in the human experience as far as the grand scheme.

We are trying, as a species, to come together within our own sense of self. We are trying to bring that spiritual awareness to the surface of our logical interpretation of who we are. And it is people like you who are willing to reach out to the divine and bring it into the physical [who] are creating the bridge for others to cross. That is what you want to see this effort as — bridge-building. That is what you are doing. You are creating bridges for those that are looking to get to the other side of this understanding of life. And you want to allow each person to find their own way in their own time to this bridge.

You must understand and respect the individual journeys of those you will come in contact with. Although you feel that this information and this kind of experience is priceless, there are many in similar situations that just can't respond in the same way, that just can't embrace this kind of idea or concept. For in the embracing of this ability to connect with someone who seems so incapable of communication, it shifts the way they view all forms of communication. And many people just aren't ready for that kind of shift in consciousness.

And so you must honor that; you must honor that each individual is exactly where they need to be, whether it be embracing you or resisting you. You must honor that, and you must give them their freedom to explore that. Do not ever try to convince anybody that needs convincing, dear one. That's not your job. You are building a bridge for those looking for a bridge. Remember that — it is not your job to convince anyone. You are simply offering a path for a new way of having this kind of experience. And as you know, each person needs to choose their own path.

I feel that you are realizing the intensity of my communication here, and I feel that it's important for you to know this ahead of time. It is important for you to realize that not everyone will embrace this as fully as you and I have. For what I know is that there are many, men especially, that are going to come at you from that logical viewpoint that I once was so good at. I understand that you are aware of how to be around that and that's where I want you to go, to that place of acceptance that if this were my Peter, fifteen, twenty years ago, we wouldn't be having this conversation, would we? We wouldn't even be considering it! And that is something that you accepted of me.

And, that's all I want to bring to your attention is that acceptance that once somebody comes at you in a most attacking manner, realize that it is you that is attacking their understanding of who they are, and who their loved one is, and their loved one's inability to communicate. You are attacking that belief system that they must just sit by and watch their loved one struggle in a physical body that does not respond in the way that they think it should.

Remember this, dear one, you will be engaging people in emotional upheaval and people can get quite defensive regarding their belief systems. Continually remind yourself that's not your job. You're not here to change anybody's belief system, only enhance the journeys of those that are seeking a truth beyond the limited, fearful interpretations that are already put forth.

I am, in this moment, experiencing a shift in my own ability to connect and communicate in the physical, and I want you to hear this. I want you to know this. I want you to know that as the human beings continue to expand and open up to this interdimensional communication, that the souls here in spirit respond accordingly. And, what that means is it is as if our energetic frequencies are beginning to come into alignment in a way that is going to affect the collective experience on a grand scale. And where individuals, such as you and I, will begin to commune on a much more regular basis, as if it is just expected that we are in constant communication, constant conversation, if you will.

And these veils that they speak of are getting thinner and thinner the more our energies come into alignment. So, what you are feeling is not insignificant, and I want you to realize that. It is true that we are becoming closer and closer; that our ability to communicate is becoming clearer and clearer; that I do speak through you; and that you have given me that opportunity to allow so much of my insights to come through you. And that is what you've been collecting … isn't it? … my insights, my inspirations. That is what you have been putting down in information form. Keep believing, my dear, for the more you believe in the moment you receive the insight, the stronger our connection becomes, and I know you are realizing this.

I know as we move further and further away from the day of my actual physical transition that you are becoming more and more aware of how expansive I truly am. And I don't want you to begin to question our connection if I shift into a more expansive expression of who I am. Right now, I am able to slip into your awareness through my identity as Peter. But there is a part of me that looks to remain in the expanse of who I am, a part of me that looks for you to reach even higher in your awareness and acceptance of who I am as the complete and total being that I am. I feel that it's important for you to see it this way, where you can begin to see this identity of Peter as only a partial representation of who I am as the soul that I am.

And it has been these past few years, when you have been able to tap into the more expansive aspect of who I am. It has been a process, if you will, of expansion in your own mind, where the first step was believing that you were connecting with my soul while my physical body was still alive.

The second step was communing with me once my body had given in, to the transition. And now that we have mastered this aspect of our communication, we are moving into a means of communication that is more interactive. That's what I want to say that there will be moments in the twilight when we meet together in the stillness, where you will feel as though you are sitting with me, you are sitting in my energy, you are sitting in my presence.

And then this will expand into something even greater where you will begin to see those images of me become clearer and clearer. I am planting these seeds in your mind so your mind begins to become comfortable with this idea that our ability to communicate is going to continue to get stronger and clearer, and begin to be integrated into the five senses that we have deemed our physical senses.

You see, nothing is really separate; nothing is truly separate. Our ability to see in the spiritual realm is defined in part by humans as … I'll say … like the third-eye chakra being our connection to the divine. Many people feel that that is where the visions can be seen, in the area of the third eye, and yet, see the distance here between what is considered the third eye and what are considered the two eyes that you see the physical world through. And realize that as we begin to merge with our higher aspects that these areas of our physicality will shift as well, that our entire being is shifting. Everything is shifting in frequency. Everything is elevating. And so if our ability to communicate elevates, well then our ability to see one another will shift accordingly.

Tara: Peter, your spiritual insights are truly illuminating. I am reading a book that a friend, Barbara, recommended regarding communing one-on-one without a medium. I believe we can have this same experience. Do you agree?

Peter: I believe in divine intervention, my dear, and I know that's something for you to be applauded. I see that there are no coincidences on Earth, so yes, this book was meant to open that idea in you, in your mind. You see, we've already had that creative energy in there, and it has always been the logical understanding of life that has kept us from fully embracing it. So when you read things like this, you begin to believe that it's possible. And once you begin to believe that it's possible, well then that energy can come forward in a much more natural and graceful way. So yes, my dear, it's not a coincidence. This is exactly how we, here in spirit, maneuver the earth plane to support your journey. Can you see how random it was to have that experience and to be in the presence of this information, and yet how perfect and divine?

Laura: Tara, whoever gave you that book was an angel in disguise.

Peter: There are many other books. There is much information regarding how to open up more, how to extend yourself to spirit more, and how to allow the energy to define the direction that you take this kind of connection. Each person waking up to this inclination now has a unique way of experiencing it. And so that's

what you want to remember. You can read others' books because it will open your mind to other possibilities, and that's important.

It's important for you to continue to realize how many *new* experiences people are having, how many *new* ways people are finding their way to connecting with a loved one. For quite some time, people thought it was only through those special few that were able to communicate, but now people are waking up en masse through their own experiences and the experiences of others. Just look around for all of the books written regarding near-death experiences or experiences where their loved ones are connecting with them from the beyond. They are not about going to a medium. They are talking about one-on-one interdimensional communication, and that is what you are opening up to. That is what this experience has been about for you. For your part, your role in this is to be able to open up and expand yourself.

And the brilliance is in this journey, my dear. The brilliance is in our ignorance prior to my illness and how the illness triggered this kind of journey of exploration, and how each step you took you expanded in your ability to believe what could be possible. And then you would take another step and realize, *well, that was possible; now let's see what else could be possible.* And that's where it's taking you on this journey. And so you realize that there is not an end to this kind of a journey. There is no ultimate goal. We just want to continue to expand our ability to find new ways to connect. It's quite an interesting and excitable journey, isn't it? It's definitely one to be born for.

Tara: Peter, thank you so much. It is an exciting adventure for us to pursue.

Peter, is my maternal grandmother still with you as she was when you made your transition?

Peter: There is something I want to bring to light so that you get a clearer understanding that there is no *here and there* when you speak about spirit. We are always here, we are always present, we are always as one. We don't feel the separateness like we do on the earth plane. It's not as if she goes to visit another relative in another country and I am no longer in her presence. Our energy is always connected. It's difficult for the human being to fully grasp that concept, but it's something I want you to begin to consider; something I want you to begin to create in your mind — that if we are each a drop in the ocean and the ocean does span the entire universe, then our connection exists in that expansive state; that our awareness can be in any moment at any part of that grand ocean and at all parts of that grand ocean in any moment.

You see ... it is baffling for the human to try to figure it out. For so many people still see us as separate individuals here in spirit, as if we are individual candles creating that one light. We are not the candles; we are only the flame, and the flame is not limited to that physical structure. It is not limited to that one space. The energy is much more expansive than that.

And so, your dear Susie ... Susan is here with me always. As far as her energetic contribution to our efforts together to write this book and to share this kind of experience, she is involved in that. Is it that you feel her? Is it that you feel a different flair in the energy from time to time? For she does have some expansive awareness to add, and she is working to do that with you.

Now there are others, and I will say that quite clearly. And I know that you have moments of awareness of this, where it comes in a much more direct manner with less emotion attached to it. And when you feel that, and you feel the sturdiness of that energy, you can know that it is your guides coming to you. For they come to you with great strength, with great integrity, and with a great sense of support.

And they are the ones that create the bridge to the collective consciousness. You see, I can do that, but from a limited perception for I still remain intact as far as my perception of life as Peter, at least as Peter the one who has experienced this life. But they have this ability to traverse the great ravines that exist between the body, mind, ego and soul, and they are able to truly assist us in this process of communication. There is always a bridge, and for us the guides create that bridge. The guides create that opportunity for you and I to connect as though we were sitting in each other's presence. They create that frequency that allows me and you to meet there, right there in the middle.

I am diligently working to affect great change to create an openness so that these new concepts can be integrated and so that you can receive the full benefits of integrating this kind of information. So please, my dear, do not hesitate to ask any question that comes. I want you to know that if a question surfaces in your mind, there is relevance regardless of how unimportant you think it is to me. If it is something that comes up in you, there is a reason, and there is a purposeful energy to assist you in creating an awareness because of the question.

Tara expresses regret that although she was in their home and fully embraced Peter's transition, at his moment of transition, she was not sitting at his side and felt frightened by the pain of parting. She felt an urge to escape the moment. The expectation of their last precious moments was highly emotional and fearful, even though, there was a knowingness that it was a transition and not the end of their evolution as souls.

Peter: Well, what I would say to that, my dear, is there could have been no wife that could have given greater support in this transitional experience than you. And you must look at the entire picture, not the moment, my dear, the entire picture. And when you see that entire picture, you cannot doubt your support of my transitional process. For you understand that this entire experience has been just that, a transitional process, and you were there for every step of it. And it was our choice as souls to experience it in this way. I honored what we agreed to as the souls that we were. I did not mean to slip out the back if you will; I did not mean to trick you in any way. I just honored what it was our souls agreed to.

There could never be a wife that could support a human being going through such a transition with such grace and dedication as you. And so you must remember that in that moment, there was nothing but bliss for me, and I did not need anything further from anyone in the physical. And I feel that if you were sitting there, I may have been more focused on your reaction to the process than my experience. I would have been, as I always have, aware of what it was you were feeling, what it was you were thinking, and how it was you were having this experience. And for both of us, we knew it had to be fully embraced, that I had to experience it in the way that I did, with no attachment to the physical. And that was the gift that you gave me. We planned it that way — I want you to know that. There is no reason for doubt, for fear, shame or guilt. It is all exactly as it was meant to be, my dear, for many, many reasons; some that I can explain to you like I just did, and some that we just have to accept as part of the divine plan.

Tara: Yes … thank you, Peter … that is a very beautiful way to put it. I love you.

Peter, would your soul be willing to speak (through a channel with Laura and me) to a small group at a presentation once our book has been published? And is it a good idea to include some lighthearted, amusing stories about your family dog, Roquefort (who passed many years ago), affording the guests some laughter? Also, Peter, I'd like to know if you know Roquefort in the spirit world?

Peter: First, I want to say that there is no difference here in the energy regarding our souls. These dogs are just as much a part of the collective as we are. Yes, they have their own morphic fields, their own resonance, but they truly do come back and forth, in and out of the physical plane as much as we do. And I, of course, know him on this level, which is why I adored him so when I was there in the physical.

I see how people can become so attached to that energy for it's so very healing. These animals, they truly are pure spirit; they are pure energy of divinity when they come to the Earth. They don't get lost and caught up in that logical interpretation of life, so they allow you to just be who you feel you are in a moment. That is the beauty of these creatures. And I would say that it's important for you to bring a lightheartedness to these gatherings, to these groups, for it is an intense subject for most human beings, and it is going to be quite emotional for many. And so, of course, humor always assists in integrating truths that are difficult for the mind to embrace.

As far as Laura and you, I see this as a wonderful joining. I see this as a creative endeavor you can experience and expand upon together.

You want to remember that people aren't going to recognize me as much as they're going to recognize their own loved ones. So, as we begin to show people how it is done,

you are then going to want to invite others to have that kind of experience with their own intimates, so that they can feel the significance of the truths being imparted. That's the most important thing.

You remember that the words weren't what got you. It was the *feeling* behind the words, the energetic connection that occurs somewhere inside of you that opens up something inside of you, opens up that sense of knowing. And so you will be an example, or we, rather, will be an example of what could be. Then you are going to want to allow others to have that similar experience, to validate for their selves and for those watching that these two energies are very different ... meaning, mine and the soul of their intimate.

Tara talks about Peter making an appearance on the earth plane to give her a sense of his presence, perhaps in the small creatures of the earth.

Peter: I am able to, but I have not felt the affinity there. I thought I might engage it more than I feel that I need to. I thought it would be a nice way to give your body, mind and ego a significant confirmation of my being-ness, but it doesn't seem to be necessary. I will, in fact, give you a sense of my presence in that way, especially now as the creatures begin to awaken en masse. But I will say that I find it more exciting to do the one-on-one thing with you, to commune together as the human representations of our souls in the way that we are doing. I choose to give my energy over to expanding this connection. And although I know it's nice to get a sign here and there, I know that I am still going to fill your mind with confirmations in many different ways. I do not want to give it away; I *do* want you to be as in awe of the experience as I am.

And I want you to know that I am in continual awe of the way that this is all playing out. I am continually gasping at the means and modes of communication available to me, like having these kinds of synchronistic experiences, like with the book. There are just so many avenues for this interdimensional communication that I am just exploring each and every one of them. I know the easier ones, the easier more predominant ways are through the butterflies and such. They are just such a gentle and spiritual energy; it makes it simple to just jump in and out. I will say that.

And, of course, the dogs do have an affinity for this kind of energy. They do allow themselves to be portals for our energy at times. And I think that it is just a part of what I knew when I was there, that a part of that animal was just so connected to a part of me beyond anything I could explain. I felt a communing with my dear Roquefort that I did not feel with many human beings. And that again, I reiterate, is because of his integrity, because of his ability to remain in constant communication with the divine. That's what they do — they're constantly in communication with the divine. They are constantly moved by the inspirational energy they feel from the connection they have to spirit and their willingness to remain open and never dismiss what they know.

They try to teach us that, you know, but we are so caught up in the idea that we know better, that we couldn't possibly learn from such a simple creature [laughter]. And I do find that quite humorous now that I see it from this point of view. So many of the creatures on the earth plane are so much wiser and so much more connected than the human being is. It's quite humorous to see the ego telling the human being that they are superior to all other creatures. But, I digressed ....

I want to remain in constant contact with you, so I will give a greater effort over to those little ones that do scurry about around you and that show themselves to you in demonstrative ways. I will get your attention. It will not be something where you will even doubt it. You will know because what you see and what you feel from within will connect. We'll make that connection, and you will have that certainty and that sense of knowing. And it's important for you to have that so that you can begin to build upon that. So, of course, I will continue to give my effort over in that direction as well.

Tara: Peter, I find it absolutely amazing that we are experiencing our journey on this interdimensional level. I am deeply grateful for your ability to reach me.

Tara [to Laura]: Do my guides have any messages for me?

Peter: I want to just remind you to give yourself equal credit for this experience. I want it to be equal; I want us both to be recognized equally for our efforts here. It's so important for you to feel that way. It's important to me that you recognize that none of this could be possible without you, my dear. You must continue to remind yourself of that. I am not the magical one. I am not the mystical one. I am not the teacher; we are learning this together. It truly is our truth. I would not be where I am in my evolution if it were not for you. So you must recognize that we are going through this experience together, and each new insight that comes through me to you expands in me my awareness of what is possible on this physical plane. Although you may not see me in a physical form, I'm still a part of this physical world experience because of you and your willingness to remain connected to me regardless of what the current overwhelming logical understanding of this experience is.

I would say that as far as the guides go, you are in perfect alignment. You are truly opening up in a way that they themselves, are responding to. So I would not say that it is too important to feel as though they have some significant message for you other than anything that came through here today. They too want to give you a sense of your perfection, of your divinity, of your grace and elegance, and of how important it is for you to realize that and honor that. That I would say is the most important thing they look to impart to you. And I can be a stand-in here for you for that is who I work with when I come to you. I work through your guides. They create that bridge, as I said before. So I want you to know that this is a cohesive movement we are all making together, to assist in the expansion of the collective conscious understanding of who we are as souls in the physical.

I love you, my dear. I love you eternally, endlessly, and limitlessly, and I will always be a part of you, and you will always be a part of me. And we will always grow together, evolve together, and love each other from a place of knowing beyond the physical.

Tara: Peter, it's too beautiful. I feel exalted by your soul's message. Communing with our thoughts and emotions is an elegant form of communication. Replete with love.

Laura: Yes, beautiful. Thank you, Peter.

[End of session/ tape.]

Chapter 24

Transcript of August 25, 2014

(Approximately Nine Months after Peter's Transition)
Channeled by Laura Mirante, Channel/Medium

Tara: My dear, wonderful Peter, I am *always* in limitless gratitude for this opportunity to meet with you soul-to-soul. I am touched deeply, by our continuing ability to create our life together in a place beyond the physical. I love you, and yes, I miss you very much.

Tara gives Peter the platform.

The following channeled transcription 'excerpts'
have been recorded and transcribed verbatim:

Peter: I will tell you that it is absolutely incredible to be a part of your experience and to be aware of the awareness you hold of me as a part of your experience. That's where the true gift lies, dear one, is in your awareness of my presence in your experience. It's as if you feel me; it's as if you recognize me; it's as if you see me. And that's something to say for those there in the physical who don't normally recognize just the presence. If they recognize the presence, they don't actually give it form in their mind. They don't actually say: *"Well, this presence, this energy reminds me of a feeling I once had with my dear loved one."*

You see, just in those recollections you make connections in the energy, in the energy of the spiritual awareness and the energy of the mental body. And that's where the connections need to be made, for this time in history is defined by the merging of spirit and physicality, by the merging of the higher awareness and the logical understanding. That is what this is all about. We are taking people to higher levels of awareness. We are asking them to expand in their logical minds what our true potential is as spiritual beings.

There will not be availability in every human being to hear what it is you are putting forth as your truth. For as you know, there are different souls at different points on their journey, different energies experiencing different levels of consciousness, just different states of perception. In those states of perception are filters, limitations, and confinements of awareness in order to perpetuate the experience. We can't all know everything, for if we did, we would be in the energy of the divine, and we wouldn't have the physical experience. The physical experience is about exploration, and it will continue as long as there is more to explore. With that understanding, you can appreciate the idea that there are individuals here at many different levels of consciousness, with many different varied understandings of who we are, varied interpretations of death, dying, and the spiritual energy that exists within and beyond this physical experience.

We need to see each other beyond the physical. We need to know each other beyond our intellectual interpretations and perceived limitations of the human beings that we are. It is how we will begin to shift the way we view one another, to shift the way we feel about one another, and to shift the way we feel about our responsibility to one another. For when you really begin to honor the truth that there is no separation, you begin to realize that when you hurt another, you do hurt yourself, and when you help another, you help yourself. And that the more you help others, the more you help this collective experience, the more that good comes back to you — to we, to the one that we are, to the energy: the creative energy that is ours to define and be defined by.

You are existing in a manner that is supported by spirit, for the manner you are existing in supports spirit. It's a way of existing that is so freeing, so fabulous and filled with wonderment. There are so many fascinating inclinations of the energy that you are becoming aware of. You really are taking a step back from life and allowing it to show you its magnificence. This is what our journey is all about. It's about being fully present in the moment, being fully present in the experience you are engaging without losing yourself in the past, without losing yourself in the future — just being here in the present, fully aware of how the energy around you shifts, of how the experience shifts accordingly, and, of how aware you are becoming because of your willingness to shift the way you perceive life.

You are no longer as reliant on the logical mind as you once were. You now look more to intuition than you do to the intellect, and that is certainly a step in the right direction. That is certainly a step in the direction the balance of humanity is looking to move in. So if it felt heavy, dear one, it's because you were taking that step for the collective. For you and those like you willing to live according to spirit are proving it could be done, are proving there's value to it and a sense of completeness.

And it's important that people understand that that's who we are. Beyond our human logical minds exists an expansive awareness. And isn't it funny that I had to lose my ability to use my intellect to tap into the expansive awareness. I would say, dear one, that that's a lesson worth teaching. That what's going on here in this intellectually driven society is a separation from our truth where the intellect is actually creating a boundary, a wall between who we really are and who we believe we are. And it's important for people to begin to realize that, that this heavy reliance we have on the intellect is keeping us stifled; it's keeping us separate from this expansive awareness available to us.

And, we must share with people this idea that the intellect is meant to support the intuition, and that it's time to focus on honing in on that connection to the intuition so that we can open that door and allow it to flow. People are so caught up in the intellect they don't even realize that this higher awareness is available to them. They think that their interpretation of life stops at the limits of intellect, and it doesn't, and it doesn't have to, and that's what we have proven, isn't it.

That's what we are demonstrating through this sharing of our journey. We are allowing people to see that in my most unconscious state, I was the most consciously aware that I can be. So what does that mean? What does humanity take from that? How do we change this society accordingly, so we don't need to have these experiences, so we don't need to create these physical world ailments to set us free from the confines of the mind.

Remember, dear one, we're born into this society without that. We're taught that. We're taught to think, and we're taught how to think, and the way we're thinking in this society is inhibiting our true spiritual awareness, or our ability to tap into that spiritual awareness. So what do we do with that? Well, we share it. We share all we know about how it took moving away from the intellect. It took calming the fears to be able to create the opening to tap into this awareness.

These are expansive concepts that are not readily available in the human mind. When those that rely so heavily on the intellect come up against some intellectual interpretation that doesn't fit into *their* intellectual interpretation — well, they tend to refute it. They also tend to feel offended by it, because if it doesn't fit and they believe they are highly intellectual, then it must be nonsense. For if it's not nonsense they have to question what they have placed great certainty in, which is their own interpretation. And most people don't want to do that. Most people don't want to doubt what they think they know, especially when they've created a life around it, especially when they've espoused that as truth.

It's going to take people time to allow themselves to integrate this information. I am only bringing to your awareness what I see in the future as far as the receptiveness of this culture and this society. But it will be grand, it will be glorious, it will be magnificent for it is you and I extending ourselves into this collective with no limitations, with no fears, completely exposed. It is our truth, and it is what we are allowing others to experience because of our willingness. It will be nothing short of wonderful, my dear, nothing short of wonderful.

I feel young, I feel innocent, and I feel curious. I feel like a child, my dear. I feel like a child, a curious child looking to explore and share and feel joy. I have you to thank for opening this door, for giving me this platform, for allowing me to realize how expansive I truly am. I have you to thank for that. With all that I am, I love you, and with all that I will ever be, I honor you.

Tara: Thank you, Peter, for those touching words. I am so grateful for your beautiful energy and all of the gifts of knowledge that you continue to bring to me. Thank you for sharing with me your youthful state in the spirit world, and how it fuels your desires to explore and create our journey with great joy!

Stepping into this well of wisdom that is available to us all has been the most magnificent experience I have known. *Our Grand Journey of Self-Exploration* fulfills our legacy; it is our truth.

I honor your soul, Peter, and the unsuspected wisdom of the Divine that has blessed us with this grand journey.

[End of session/tape.]

We will continue together to experience life in the physical, as two souls committed to one another and devoted to the exploration of self.

Chapter 25

Explore New Ways

It has only been about one hundred years since people had no problem believing in the spirit world and depending upon self-healing resources. I am thankful for the methods now available, whether new or resurfacing from ancient knowledge. Our challenges can be an exciting adventure if we open our hearts and minds to the possibilities available and affect the collective experience on a grand scale.

Peter's step-by-step transition made it possible for me to have the stability needed to transition into writing our book jointly. We have taken the experiences of our grand journey to a new level by showing others who are willing to embrace our story that they can communicate with their loved ones in spirit. With respect to all spiritual lives, Peter and I have created a bridge for those who are willing to get to the other side of this understanding of life. *Our Grand Journey of Self-Exploration* is a guidebook to how to maneuver through the human experience with an awareness that will allow you to rise above the human experience. Use your energetic power for an opportunity to internalize and experience the wisdom behind these words.

You can now sidestep the difficulties and challenges that Peter and I had to take to be driven from the intellectual understanding of who we are and to be set free from the limitations of the intellectual interpretation. Beyond our logical minds exists an expansive awareness. Peter had to lose the ability to use his intellect so he could tap into this expansive awareness. That is a lesson worth learning. One does not have to go through what Peter did to live a life of love, peace, joy and harmony. Our awareness does not stop at the limits of the intellect, and that is what we have demonstrated through this sharing of our journey. We have allowed our readers to see that in Peter's most unconscious state, he was the most consciously aware that he could be.

Becoming knowledgeable about our continuing evolution beyond the body, mind and ego increases our awareness of life beyond the physical body. We are spiritual, conscious beings; we are not a physical body, for the human is just a temporary state. The journey from the physical realm to the spiritual realm is a reality that cannot be escaped.

There are approximately sixteen different ways to communicate with a loved one spiritually, in the physical realm and the afterlife. It is part of the human experience to be able to create a different observation on the planet by manifesting a new reality for yourself. This reality is a greater reality beyond our five senses and human self. Open the door to a deeper understanding of who we are as a soul … the soul that never leaves us.

The following list is a few of many available resources:

Afterlife Communication: 16 Proven Methods, 85 True Accounts by R. Craig Hogan, Ph.D, Gary E. Schwartz, Ph.D, Sonia Rinaldi, MA, and Suzanne Giesemann, MA. Greater Reality Publications, 2014.

Wolf Message by Suzanne Giesemann, MA. Waterside Productions, Incorporated, 2014.

Your Eternal Self by R. Craig Hogan, Ph.D. Greater Reality Publications, 2008.

The Afterlife Experiments: Breakthrough Scientific Evidence of Life After Death by Gary Schwartz, Ph.D, Deepak Chopra, MD and William L. Simon. Atria Books reprint edition, 2003.

A Bridge to Healing: J.T.'s Story by Sarina Baptista. Bridge to Healing Press, 2nd edition, 2014.

The Jewel in the Condition by Cindy Collins Sparkman. Green Parrot Press, 2007.

Flip Side: A Tourist's Guide on How to Navigate the Afterlife by Richard Martini. Homina Publishing, 2011.

Guided Afterlife Connections by Rochelle Wright, MS and R. Craig Hogan, Ph.D. Greater Reality Publications, 2013.

Everyone must find their own way ... each seeker is a path to himself.

Chapter 26

About the Author

Tara O'Toole-Conn was a social science and art major at Rutgers University in New Jersey and Florida International University. She began her career as a legal assistant with several prestigious Pittsburgh- and Philadelphia-based law firms. She is a former painter, ceramist, and sculptor. She takes pleasure in many music genres, theater, reading, and journaling. She has an ongoing passion for human and spiritual development; she is an Usui Reiki Master and a Pilates enthusiast.

A native of Pittsburgh, Pennsylvania, Tara now resides in Louisville, Kentucky. She is the widow and former caregiver for her beloved husband, Peter D. Conn. She had no former expertise in caregiving or the field of spiritual communications. It was the human, compromised suffering her husband remained in for years preceding his transition that brought her to the pages of *Our Grand Journey of Self-Exploration*. Her immense gratitude goes to Peter for their spiritual and human experiences of the past decade as they journeyed a life through illness.

May you always be guided by the light of your
dreams and the music in your heart.

Printed in the United States
By Bookmasters